SNATCHING JOY

'CAUSE SOMETIMES LIFE JUST STINKS

MEGAN ANN SCHEIBNER

ISBN: 978-0-9969312-3-6

CONTENTS

STUDY QUESTIONS

DEDICATION

To My Sister Joyce ... My little sister by birth, my sister-in-Christ by rebirth, and my co-heir of the joy that is ours in Christ.

And

To Mrs. Phyllis Monroe ... You literally saved my grammatical bacon!
Thanks for crying at all the right parts.

FOREWORD

It was 1:15 AM, on June 24th, 2014. My wife of 4 years and our six-month-old baby had just landed from our flight out of Wichita. The fact that it was June 24th was significant. It was exactly three weeks and five days since the home explosion that took place in Garden City, Kansas, with my wife's mother and two brothers inside. Spencer, who was about to turn 18, had died at the scene. Bystanders had been unable to get to him in the wreckage and fire. Ten days later, 16-year-old Riley succumbed to his burns and injuries. And less than a week after that, her mother passed as we were driving back from Riley's funeral. Three funerals in three weeks. And now, feeling tired, dark, and at a late hour, we were driving home from the airport.

It honestly happened faster than I could react. One moment I was driving down the interstate; the next, a deer leaped in front of my headlights. The deer bounced off of the front passenger side of the vehicle, and I swerved as the car spun out in the middle of the highway. I'm not sure exactly how, but we came to a stop on the side of the road, inches from the guard rail. Once I caught my breath, I discovered that nobody was hurt and stepped out of the vehicle to assess the damage.

An hour later, after several phone calls to insurance and family, my mother drove up behind us to offer us a ride the rest of the way home. It was at this moment that an unlikely source taught me an unexpected lesson in joy. As my mother reached into the backseat and lifted my six-month-old infant out of her seat, Kaleigh greeted her grandmother with the purest smile. I saw in her eyes radiant joy at seeing this person she loved. Kaleigh saw the flashing lights, how dark it was, and we knew she was tired. Yet, in the midst of that, she chose joy. The truth is, she had been trying to teach me this lesson for the last several weeks. As everyone in Kansas had been living with a mix of grief at the losses, and dread of the doctors' certain words that Kelly and Riley wouldn't make it, Kaleigh had been smiling joyfully. While sitting in her car seat in the hospital, Kaleigh would stop what she was doing to greet every visitor with a smile. I was worried about my car, and my wife was exhausted from our long journey. But even at this moment, Kaleigh taught us that we could choose joy.

I don't know why you picked up this book. Maybe you're like me, sitting on the side of a highway, unable to find joy at the moment. Maybe joy seems like a foreign concept in your world. But I can promise you, joy lies at the end of the line, amid the storm, at the tip of the spear. No matter your circumstances, I hope that this book allows you to find joy, and never let it go.

Peter Scheibner

LET'S CHAT

Have We Met?

Hi there!

Some of you are already, my dear friends. We've met in person, or through my books, or on social media. For others, however, you may be wondering just who I am.

In a nutshell, I'm Megan Scheibner!

I'm a husband-hugger to Steve, and I'm 'Mom' to the eight kids with the last name of Scheibner and more non-Scheibner kids than I can count. I'm a grandma to seven–so far–grandkids. I love to read and write and cook and organize anything not nailed down.

I have an undergrad degree in Speech Communications, (My folks used to claim I was vaccinated with a phonograph needle. Perhaps they were right!). My Master's degree is in Christian Ministry with a focus on Biblical Counseling, and I'm currently pursuing my Doctorate of Marriage and Family Counseling.

My husband Steve and I run the Characterhealth Ministry, so much of my time is producing resources and traveling to teach about marriage, parenting, and discipleship. Honestly, discipleship floats my boat! You'll get to know that and me better in these pages, but for now, let me assure you that I'm a fellow-traveler on this spiritual journey. Somedays, I've got it reasonably well put together, but other days I'm just a mess!

I can't wait to get to know you through these pages, and I sure hope you'll join me for the accompanying online study. We've got so much to learn about joy, and I'm excited to learn right alongside you.

And now, a note just for you ...

Dear sister in Christ,

Can I tell you just how awesome you are?

Truly, there is no end to your dedication. You're dedicated to so many good and worthwhile things: loving your families, caring for your homes, fulfilling your many daily responsibilities. Add to that your relationship to Christ and your dedication to consistently spending time in the Word, your faithfulness to prayer and Scripture memorization. You diligently serve others while trying to squeeze in some precious time for life-giving fellowship and friendships. Your lives are filled to full and over-flowing!

I totally get it. But, I'm afraid that in the midst of our dedication, we have a problem. As women who thrive on *doing* what is right, all of those areas of dedication can simply become checks in the block as we try to quantify, schedule, and plan for obedient living.

But what about being joyful?

God's command for His children to exhibit joy in their daily lives is just as crystal clear as His call to obedience in every other area of life. But, how in the world do we add joyfulness to our already over-crowded lives? Is it something that we pencil into our busy to-do lists? Where does joy fit into our hectic lives of mothering, cleaning, creating, chauffeuring, and being the all-around *I've Got It* go-to-person?

Where does joy fit into days, and weeks, and sometimes even months or years that are just plain HARD? Let's be honest about it ... Sometimes our circumstances just stink! We wonder when the relentless pressure will stop and will we ever smile again. For some of us, we feel a bit ripped off. After all, wasn't this Christian thing supposed to make life easier? Where's the sunshine and daffodils of the joyful Christian life?

After many years of discipling and spending time counseling with women from all over the country and from every season of life, one thing has become very apparent to me ... For many women, joy is elusive. Although we have moments, and perhaps even seasons, of what we would consider to be joy, too often that joy seems to slip away, and we're left wondering where it went. And perhaps more importantly, wondering if we will ever find it again.

Which leads to some important questions:

- Is it inevitable that our lives will always consist of joyful peaks, followed by joyless valleys?
- Must joy be fleeting?
- Is joy something slippery and destined to fall just beyond our grasp?
- Must we manufacture and whip up joy within ourselves?
- Is joy even necessary to live a fulfilled Christian life?

This little book is meant to answer those questions and more. As we study the definition of joy, the Source of joy, and the Biblical requirements to make joy our daily decision, I believe that we will discover a wellspring of joy bubbling up in our own hearts. Even more so, as we recognize the power of joy, as exhibited through obedient daily choices, we'll begin the exciting journey of grasping, internalizing, and then, sharing that Christ-driven joy with others.

As we begin this walk through the Word of God, please allow me to offer you some encouragement.

First, please diligently and carefully read all of the referenced Scripture verses for yourself. As you carefully examine the topic of joy in the context of the various passages we will be studying, you will begin to develop a fuller and more comprehensive understanding of what the word JOY truly means. Don't just read the passages! Take all of the time that is necessary to meditate on those Scriptures and to think through personal applications of the Scriptures *for your own life*. Remember, even if you're completing this study with other women, their personal applications won't necessarily look like your personal applications. That's the beauty of our uniqueness in Christ and our freedom to exercise our own Christian liberty. Jot down your personal applications and include practical achievable steps to ensure positive spiritual change in your heart and actions. Trust me, only reading about joy without putting what we read into action will never produce Christlike joy in our hearts.

Secondly, as you work through each assignment, located in the back of the book, choose at least one of the verses and commit it to memory. God's Word, hidden in our hearts, is an encouragement to joyful living when we are discouraged. That carefully memorized Scripture will be used by God to rescue our hearts when discouragement, fear, or doubt rear their ugly heads. God's Word, hidden in our hearts, can provide the exhortation we need to view what seems to us like a joyless circumstance, through the eyes of God. God's Word, hidden in our hearts, is the antidote to what we will soon discover is the sin of joylessness. I promise that as we faithfully memorize these wonderful verses regarding joy, God will use them to convict, exhort, encourage, and grow us up into joy-filled and joy-spreading believers!

Finally, as you come to the end of each chapter, you will find some personal application questions. Please complete these questions before you move on to the next chapter. For those of you who are studying this book in a small group, some of the questions will be appropriate for discussion. However, don't ever feel as though you need to share what you've written. The personal application questions are just that–Personal! For most questions, I've allowed five spaces to fill in your answers. Sometimes you won't have five answers, so don't feel pressured to fill them in just to make me happy. (I hate busy work, too.) On the other hand, if you have more than five answers, record those answers wherever you can find a space to write.

Let me encourage you–exhort you, plead with you, nag you– to share what you learn about joy with others. We live in a hurting world of family, friends, co-workers, and even just acquaintances, who are desperate for the joy that comes from a right understanding of God and of His promise of joy to those who are His. As you begin to bubble over with the truths that you are learning about joy, you will both cement those truths in your own heart, as well as incite a hunger for joy in the hearts of your friends and family. So many of the Scriptures that we will be studying will be beneficial for those who find themselves in times of trial, hurting, and darkness; be generous with the gift of the Word of God and allow Him to minister truth and joy to precious wounded hearts.

Joy doesn't have to be elusive! Instead, Christ-centered, Christ-focused, and Christ-generated joy can and should be the permanent and daily discipline of our lives. Together, let's allow the Word of God, through the Holy Spirit, to develop us into joyful and winsome women of God. When that happens, not only will we be personally blessed, but we'll also be a blessing to a watching, hurting world that needs the joy that our precious Savior offers.

This journey isn't going to be a sprint through the Scriptures. Think of it more as preparing for a marathon. Now, it's time to strap on our training shoes and stretch out our muscles. We've much ahead of us as we begin this journey toward joy!

INTRODUCTION

With all His heart and with all His soul, God joins us in the pursuit of our everlasting joy because the consummation of that joy in Him redounds to the glory of His own infinite worth. All who cast themselves on God find that they are carried into endless joy by God's omnipotent commitment to His own glory. –John Piper

Have you ever misplaced something that was precious to you? I don't know about you, but the older I get the more that seems to happen! Sometimes, I can remember that I put the missing object somewhere for safe keeping, but that *safe keeping* remains even safer when I just can't remember where it is–very frustrating and often embarrassing. Often, I don't remember putting the missing item anywhere special, and it ends up just being plain old lost with a capital L! In fact, just this past week, I pulled out ALL of my summer clothes, hung them up, and realized that my very *favoritest* skirt of all, the one I wore all last summer, was missing. It was just gone. I complained to anyone who would listen, "How does that even happen??"

One skirt seems like such a small thing, but trust me when I say that it was consuming my thoughts and bringing on Mrs. Cranky-Pants. (Or, I suppose in this case, Mrs. Cranky-Skirt) On a whim, I decided to take one last look in our storage closet. "Perhaps," I thought, "Maybe, it fell out of the box." However, it was nowhere to be found when I searched the closet. But then ... my eyes fell on our gigantic, bright neon green suitcase, and I had the vaguest memory of putting something in it. I pulled it out of the closet, unzipped the zipper, and low and behold, there was my skirt ... Plus ALL the rest of my summer clothes! I didn't even remember that I'd forgotten the rest of the wardrobe. Again, how does that even happen??

Don't judge! I realize that losing a skirt is a trivial thing. (But honestly, once you find something you like ... I know you ladies understand.) However, losing our joy is a different matter altogether. Although the outline for this study was first written four years ago as a topical study for the ladies' class that I was teaching, my study of joy really began fifteen years ago. Fifteen years ago, for the first time in my Christian walk, I found myself desperately missing the joy of my salvation, and feverishly attempting to Get. It. Back! Let me explain ...

Although I didn't grow up in a Christian home, I had a nothing-to-complain- about childhood. I experienced the usual break-up, make-up, break-up heartache of a long-term relationship in high school. I had the usual illnesses, broken bones, and unreasonable teachers that accompany growing up. I had magical experiences like working tons of hours as a waitress, so I could afford to travel with the high school band through Europe as a pom-pom girl–insert blushing face– during both my junior and senior years. I drove a bright yellow, $300.00 beater convertible that was the envy of all my friends. It was amazing how that little two-seater car could fit all my friends on the back ledge and still leave an open front seat for my on-again, off-again, on-again boyfriend!

I was pretty much just your normal, All-American girl. However, underlying all of those very normal, nothing-out-of-the-ordinary experiences, was the shadow of darkness. Looking back, I still don't know why, but I spent much of my childhood feeling like an outsider–an observer who was watching someone who looked exactly like me enjoying their life. Maybe it was because of my introverted personality, maybe it was linked to my adoption and birth family, (that's another book for another day) or maybe it was just one of the tools that God was going to use to draw me to Himself. Regardless, on the day that I trusted Christ for my salvation, although I didn't have an overly emotional response, it was as though the gloomy, joyless mask was lifted, and for the first time in my 22 years of life, I woke up each morning and walked through each day with joy over-flowing in my heart.

I can't even express how sweet that joy was to me! And miracle of miracles, it didn't ever go away! Even when I experienced my husband's long deployments with the Navy, scary medical conditions with my children, frequent uprooting, saying good-bye, and moving once again, and even the daily squabbles and skirmishes of motherhood ... The joy was always there! It was my constant companion and my daily source of strength. In fact, that joy changed me into what my husband–somewhat facetiously–calls a "Pollyanna Personality." Even during times of financial worry, when Steve shares the bleak economic *what-ifs* that we might face, my brain is automatically cataloging the ten ways that those negative situations can be a blessing. Encouraging to me; frustrating to him!

Which brings me to fifteen years ago...

In 2000, Steve accepted the call to plant a church in Northern New England. Our family moved back to an area that we had previously called home during our time in the Navy. We moved back with high hopes, big ideas, and God-given excitement. Being part of a church plant was one of the most exhilarating experiences that I had ever had. The memory of our previous time in a church plant in Corpus Christi, Texas, filled me with anticipation for this new adventure in Northern New England.

Honestly, the first five years were amazing! We watched God bring families and singles to the church who were hungry to grow. We stood amazed as young adults took ownership of their church and purposefully served each other and the church body. Steve's vision of a discipleship-focused church was producing Biblical results and we were so grateful and excited. But right around the five-year mark, things began to change, and that change produced an unexpected and unfamiliar shift in my heart and attitude. As I experienced disappointment in the moral failures of our church leadership, deep hurt from the incessant–at least it seemed that way to me– "Pastor's Wife" jokes and gossip, and uneasiness about hidden sin that I just couldn't pinpoint in the Scheibner-kid camp, my heart began to ache and my joy began to disappear.

At first, I don't think anyone else realized what was going on in my heart. I've always been pretty good at the everything-is-just-fine-how-about-you game face. Even for me, it was a gradual change, a gradual loss of joy, and a slow hardening of my heart and emotions. Soon, however, I was dragging myself downstairs each morning, simply putting in my time with the kids until I could lie down again for an afternoon nap, and falling asleep by 9:00 every evening. I was finding excuses not to leave the house and avoiding my responsibilities at church. To add to the equation, living in Northern New England meant that from late October until May, I was living in the inevitable gray of a New England winter. Sometimes it snowed. Sometimes it rained. But always, every single day it seemed to be just gray, gray, gray.

What color would you choose if you were describing joy as a color? Would it be pink, or purple, or perhaps bright orange? I think of joy as yellow like a daffodil. Or, blue like a cloudless sky. Or, green like newly-mown grass. On the other hand, joylessness, to me, is just dull gray. And not a pretty gray like Sherwin-Williams SW-6260 "Unique Gray" or SW-6261 the very aptly named "Swanky Gray." No, joylessness is just dull gray, Gray, GRAY! And that's how life felt to me ... Gray! More and more each day, I felt as though I was being crushed by sadness and enveloped by gray discouragement. The almost daily question that my husband and kids were asking me became, "Is everything ok?" Quite frankly, I wasn't even sure how to verbalize an answer.

After years of having joy as my constant companion, finding myself lost in the gray murkiness of discouragement was, quite honestly, frightening. I tried to just "fix it" myself. I read my Bible more, I prayed more, I even memorized an entire book of the Bible, but it just didn't seem to change my wandering heart. It wasn't until I began to really study my Bible, in order to discover exactly what God had to say about joy, that my heart was first convicted, then drawn to

xx   *Introduction*

obedient repentance, and finally, refilled with my sweetest friend and much-needed life-mate... Joy!

The past ten years of traveling to parenting, marriage, ladies', and homeschool conferences all around the country, has been such a gift to me. I've loved interacting with believers from all different walks of life. I've loved sharing counsel and being ministered to at the same time. However, one thing has become so clear to me during my time on the road. Wherever we travel, there is no missing the truth that so many of my sweet sisters in Christ are living with that same back-breaking, soul-crushing, deep gray joylessness of discouragement, fear, and sorrow. Whether it's because of broken family relationships, wayward children, the loss of loved ones, or just willful sin, many are muddling through days with downcast hearts.

Oh sure, we try to put on the Christian *happy face* for our families and friends, but deep in our hearts, we long for joy. We sometimes even wonder aloud, "Is this it? Is the Christian life just to be stoically endured with silent, inward gloom? Is our only hope heaven while life on earth is something simply to be endured? Is there something we're missing in this quest for joyful Christ-honoring living? Is there joy to be found in the journey of life?"

After years now of studying and putting into practice what the Scriptures have taught me about Biblical joy, I can confidently answer those questions with a resounding YES! Joy is the birthright of every child of God. Joy is a gift from our loving Father, and because it is based in His character, His Name, and the permanence of His promises, we can claim that joy as our own.

Now, before we go any further, I need to make sure that you understand my heart for all of you. I am, in **No Way** saying that we will never be unhappy! There is a big difference between joy and happiness, and there's an equally vast divide between joylessness and unhappiness. In Chapter 9, we'll examine the very real truth that joy and sadness can and do co-exist. We'll also discover how we can allow the Holy Spirit to minister to our hearts and how we can minister help and hope to the hearts of our friends as we struggle to keep unhappiness from hiding our joy from view. There is no escaping it, as long as we're trapped in these earthly bodies and living in our sinful world, it is inevitable that joy and unhappiness will co-exist. But stick with me now ... Unless we understand joy in its fullness, we'll always struggle to differentiate between the two. Laying a firm foundation of understanding and putting into practice God-promised joy is our greatest weapon against the unhappiness of our trials and hardships.

Claiming joy involves determination, self-evaluation, and a deeply held commitment to obedience. But, claiming joy is a marvelously great adventure of building faith, cultivating relationship with our God, and seeing others won to Christ as they observe the light that joy can bring to the darkest situation. Reading about joy won't change us anymore than sitting in a garage will make us a car. However, we'll see growth and change in our *lives* as we put into practice what we're learning with our *minds*.

I don't know about you, but I'm raring to go! It's time to begin our life-long adventure of **Snatching Joy: 'Cause Sometimes Life Just Stinks!**

YOU KEEP USING THAT WORD; I DON'T THINK IT MEANS WHAT YOU THINK IT MEANS

"True Christian joy is the heart's harmonious response to the Lord's song of love."– A. W. Tozer

Have you noticed that sometimes the English language just isn't very helpful? For instance, do we lie on the bed or lay on it? When you tell me that you've purchased a new bat are you talking about a piece of equipment from my favorite sport? (Go Sox!!) Or, did you buy a nasty nocturnal creature that wants to suck my blood? And don't even get me started on the word LOVE. I love my country, I love my husband, and I love chocolate cake–They can't possibly all mean the same thing ... Can they?

So, it is with the word JOY. Often, we say we've lost or we're lacking joy when what we actually mean is that we just aren't HAPPY. Although we use joy and happiness inter-changeably, the two words do not at all mean the same thing! Before you shake your head, roll your eyes at my nerdiness, and say it's just a semantical issue, let's dig a little deeper.

When law enforcement officials want to learn to recognize counterfeit bills, we might assume that they would begin their research by carefully studying some counterfeit money. If we assumed that, we would be wrong! Instead of wasting their time studying counterfeits, they study real currency to familiarize themselves with the touch, smell, look, and intricate details of the real deal. It's the same with understanding the difference between joy and happiness. Joy is the real deal and when we settle for anything less than the real deal, we will surely miss what God has graciously promised and provided for us!

Happiness comes from the root word *Hap*. In every language, going back as far as ancient Greek, the word for happiness is a cognate with the word *Luck*. In both Old Norse and Old English, happiness simply meant luck or chance. The French changed the word to *heur*, which then became *bonheur*, meaning good fortune. Whether it's luck, chance, or good fortune, the word Hap symbolizes something that is situational, and, therefore, out of our control.

Happiness is fickle because it is totally dependent on our circumstances. That's why we can be happy in one moment and overcome with sadness the next. That's why our mama-hearts can be filled with sappy happiness at the sight of our children sweetly playing together, then suddenly be transformed to irritated frustration when their happy play turns to bickering. Likewise, just think how happy we can be when we're out on a romantic date with our husband, then the sudden sharp turn that happiness can take when finances enter the conversation. For me, I can be filled with fan-girl giddy happiness when the Red Sox hit a grand slam, but that giddy happiness is quickly replaced by fan-rage anger when the umpire makes a bad call.

Joy isn't anything like happiness! Joy isn't based on circumstances but is instead formed through security. Joy is established by our eternity-promised, settled relationship with the Lord, and solely on the basis of our salvation. Joy is centered on what He has accomplished for us eternally, not on the situation in which we find ourselves in the moment. Joy is grounded and founded in the promises of God alone. Because of those promises, we can have joy permanently and with no fear of it slipping through our fingers or being snatched from our hearts.

Don't just believe me, though. The promise that we can have joy, and that our joy can be eternal is found in the Word of God. Let's consider just a couple of the promises that provide the believer with the assurance of that salvation-provided, promise-centered, God-settled joy.

First, we have the promise of our eternal salvation through the finished work of Jesus Christ. That promise began on the day of our salvation and will be carried on until we are made perfect with Christ Jesus. The promise of eternal joy is as foundational as John 3:16.

FOR GOD so loved the world that He gave His only begotten Son, that whosoever believes in Him, shall not perish, but have eternal life.

AT THE POINT that we recognized our sinful condition and cried out to God in repentance and need, we became part of that great "whosoever." Because our God is absolutely and unquestionably faithful, we can confidently trust that we will never perish, but have eternal life. Wonderfully, God didn't make that promise begrudgingly or out of obligation, but John 3:16 reminds us that He did so because of His great love for us.

The second foundational promise of our joy comes from understanding God's heart and purposes for those whom He calls sons. Interestingly, although we often quote Jeremiah 29:11 to young adults who are despairing of ever finding "*The*" one, we too often forget that this verse encapsulates God's intentional care for each and every one of His children.

"FOR I KNOW the plans I have for you," declares the Lord, "plans to prosper you and not to harm you, plans for a future and a hope."

KNOWING that a) I belong to God now and forever, and b) He has only good plans for my future, provides me with all I need to find my joy in God and in His good and perfect promises! My joy has nothing to do with my situation or my circumstances! Whether good or bad, circumstances can never provide the settled security the heart needs. Instead, that firm foundation of security is found only in the character and promises of our God.

The Declaration of Independence states that we, as citizens of the United States of America, have the inalienable right to Life, Liberty, and the Pursuit of Happiness. And we do! We have the right to pursue all of the happiness that life can bring. Within the safe boundaries of the Word of God, there is absolutely nothing wrong with seeking after happiness. However, as citizens of a heavenly kingdom, we have an even greater right. We have the right to OWN eternal joy. Why can we own it? Simply because the King of our heavenly kingdom has determined that His joy is to be our joy, as well.

The difference between the ownership of joy and the pursuit of happiness can really be summed up in a simple stewardship comparison. The stewardship of the gift of joy that we've been given by our Lord is a matter of Christian responsibility. On the other hand, the stewardship of our pursuit of happiness is a matter of Christian liberty.

Let's consider that statement from the Declaration of Independence once again. While we are given the clear right to pursue happiness, we are not told that we have the right to possess it. There is no expectation communicated that our pursuit of happiness will necessarily end successfully. We are just given the freedom to pursue those things that we would equate with happiness. My pursuit of happiness will, in all likelihood, look very different from your pursuit of happiness. (Especially if you're into things like cliff diving, mountain climbing, parasailing, and bungee jumping!)

I pursue happiness by playing games with my kids. (Let's be honest, true happiness is actually *beating* my kids at games.) I pursue happiness while feeding teenage boys and watching them return for seconds—and sometimes—even thirds. I pursue happiness as I sit on the beach and simply watch the waves, while listening to their crashing roar. I pursue happiness when I go to Fenway Park, watch the Red Sox win, and leave the stadium singing along to the happy sound of their victory song, "Muddy Waters." But ... Sometimes, my pursuit of happiness through game playing is thwarted by sarcastic put-downs that turn our fun into wounded feelings. Sometimes, I burn the cookies. Other times, I must flee the beach because storm clouds are rolling in. And perhaps worst of all, more often than I'd like, my wonderful Red Sox lose!

None of these happiness pursuits are sinful. In fact, they all fall well within the boundaries of my Christian liberty. They don't violate the Word of God and they don't cause me to stumble in my testimony. However, these pursuits are not a right and should never become an expectation. Joy, on the other hand, is our right as children of God. The expectation of joy is that as beloved children of God, we will steward His gift of joy-filled living with careful responsibility and faithful oversight.

Understanding the difference between joy and happiness will help us in our relationships with others, as well. Again, since joy is meant to be owned by every Christian, we have the privilege and obligation to point our Christian friends back to the foundation of joy when trials rear their ugly heads. However, since happiness is pursued differently by different Christians, we have no right to insist that our friends follow along with us in our pursuit of happiness. In fact, while the stewardship of happiness through Christian liberty may allow you to enjoy certain hobbies or activities, for your Christian friend, those same pursuits may be a stumbling block or something that feeds a harmful sin-appetite. I worked with young adults for many, many years and too often, I witnessed the convictions of one young adult being maligned by the group when that one chose not to join in the same pursuits of happiness as everyone else. To me, one of the greatest Christian freedoms we enjoy is the freedom to uphold another believer's convictions, even if we do not hold those same convictions for ourselves.

Let me share one more illustration about the difference between joy and happiness before we move on. If you're a member of the Scheibner family, you can be sure that when you arrive home for Thanksgiving, there will be a piece of apple pie with your name written on it. We are an apple pie eating bunch! Just for a moment, think of that apple pie as the gift of joy. All on its own, apple pie is delicious, fulfilling, and a really special treat. Everyone in my family starts with the same, equal-sized slice of apple pie. However, what happens next is very different for each family member. Steve eats his pie with a chunk of cheddar cheese. Baleigh gobbles hers with whipped cream. Peter wolfs his down with vanilla ice cream. Taylor devours his with a drizzle of warmed caramel sauce. And me? I daintily nibble on mine with a gigantic scoop of chocolate ice cream with hot fudge liberally poured over the top. Just to fit in, I also sometimes add whipped cream and a drizzle of caramel–No judgment, please!

If that apple pie represents the gift of joy, our diverse toppings are the happiness we seek in addition to our original slice of pie. In the end, each dessert plate looks different from the others. And that's okay! All are well within their rights to pursue apple pie happiness in whatever way seems best to them. We all have that liberty, and none of us has stepped over the parameters of the Word of God. (Well, except for maybe, possibly, perhaps me... I suppose that what I concoct might be considered gluttony.)

But what if on one particular Thanksgiving, all we had to share was just the pie? Would we moan and complain and say that life isn't fair? I hope not! The truth of the matter is that the apple pie, even with no other adornments, is still delicious, fulfilling, and a special treat. Now, before you begin to overthink this illustration, I realize that it breaks down in many areas: The pie gets eaten, what happens when the pie is gone, can we save some of the pie for later? Please, just stick with me. ☺

Like that pie, our joy is sweet and fulfilling. Yes, we have the freedom to pursue life's happy moments. However, even if we never experienced another moment of earthly happiness, our secure, settled, eternal joy is enough. In fact, such joy is more than ample to fill our hearts and to overflow from our lives.

The mighty chasm between happiness and joy is vast! While happiness is totally dependent on circumstances, joy depends on a relationship. That relationship is our relationship with the Lord Jesus Christ. Like our salvation, then, joy is a gift to us from God, Himself. True abiding joy always and only comes from our settled relationship with Jesus, and it is ours for the here and now, as well as for eternity.

Dr. Jim Berg, while writing about marriage, shares this wonderful truth about our relationship with God because of Christ Jesus.

MARRIAGE WAS CREATED by God to mirror the kind of relationship He wishes to have with us. God intends for couples to become 'one flesh'. Lovers are those who have mutual intimacy; the relationship is primarily about each other. Lovers find their greatest joy to be the joy of the other. The kind of relationship God has in mind for us will mean that both the Creator and the creature find their greatest joy in the joy of the other.

THE AWESOME TRUTH of that type of love relationship is almost more than our feeble human minds can comprehend. Think about it, as we find joy in our relationship with God, He finds joy in His relationship with us. Such intimate fellowship begins and ends with God alone and is only made possible because of His supreme and sacrificial love for us ... His children!

To keep things simple, here's my one-sentence definition of biblical joy that we'll be referencing throughout this book:

BIBLICAL JOY IS *the inner attitude and outward actions that reflect rejoicing in God's salvation and promises regardless of our outward circumstances: One of the fruits of a right relationship with God.*

BECAUSE THIS JOY IS A GIFT, we cannot, in actuality, lose our joy. We can, however, misuse it or choose to define it inappropriately. In fact, we can even claim to have had our joy robbed or stolen from us due to our circumstances, although in truth, that just isn't possible because of the permanence of God's gift to us.

Happiness is a meager substitute for true Biblical joy! We mustn't ever allow our pursuit of happiness or disappointment over hard circumstances to blind us to the beauty of the joy that is ours because of Christ. Even on the days when joy seems distant, our ownership is sure because of God's promises to us. To be a believer is to be a possessor of joy.

PERSONAL APPLICATION:

- Although we'll dig into this topic more in a later

chapter, may I encourage you right now to
compile a simple list of the current
circumstances that seem to be threatening your
joy? Changing your vocabulary concerning
circumstances is an important first step in
recognizing their limited dominance. No
circumstance can rob you of your joy.
Circumstances just don't have that kind of power.
Your happiness ... That can absolutely be stolen
away. But, *not* your joy. Retraining our minds,
hearts, and words to reflect the permanence of
our joy will help us to cling to that joy when
happiness is fleeting.

- Choose one of the verses studied in this chapter
  and commit it to memory. I find it helpful to
  write out the verse on one side of a notecard with
  the reference on the other. Stick it in your purse
  and spend a few moments reviewing whenever
  you get the chance.

2

WE'RE NOT THE FIRST TO WALK
THIS ROAD

W*e can state the gospel clearly; we can smell unsound doctrine a mile away. If asked how one may know God, we can at once produce the right formula: that we come to know God through Jesus Christ the Lord, in virtue of his cross and mediation, on the basis of his word of promise, by the power of the Holy Spirit, via a personal exercise of faith. Yet, the gaiety, goodness, and unfetteredness of spirit which are the marks of those who have known God are rare among us.*

— J. I. Packer

I'M NOT sure if this is a comforting thought or one that just saddens me, but this feeling of *losing our joy* isn't something that's entirely new to this generation of believers. The early church dealt with the same feelings of losing a joy that they had once so eagerly embraced. They, too, wondered how to continue on when their joy seemed to have disappeared.

For a long time, I thought to myself, "How could they?" After all, they had the apostles available to share in-person stories of their time with Jesus. Many of the early believers had been witnesses to both the Resurrection and the events of Pentecost. They were experiencing and witnessing unexplainable miracles. Yet still, they stumbled in their joy and succumbed to joylessness. I really couldn't understand how they could be lacking in joy.

But here's a hard truth ... Although we may not have been witnesses to the historical events of the early church, unlike those early believers, we have access to the Word of God. We have written records of God's faithfulness to the generations of Christians who have walked before us. We have personally seen God answer prayer and change lives. Yet, we too, stumble in our joy. We take our eyes off Jesus, focus on our trials, and lose sight of our God-given gift of joy. What is it that causes us to be such forgetful followers? As always, the Scripture has the answer.

I'm not sure that I would have wanted to be a member of the Galatian church when the letter from the Apostle Paul arrived in town! I don't know about you, but usually I think of Paul as a reasonably gentle teacher. In the book of Galatians, however, he reminds me of Clint Eastwood in an old-time Western. He, through the words and tone of his letter, came riding into town, brandishing the truth of the Gospel like a loaded six-shooter! He had something to say to the Galatian believers, and he didn't waste any time getting to the point. Unlike those old-time Westerns, he didn't need to get 20 shots from his six-shooter to get his point across to his readers. All he needed was the truth of the Gospel to rebuke, remind, and return the Galatians to the freedom that was to be found in Christ.

The book of Galatians is remarkable because of some notable exceptions in the writing style of Paul. First of all, he begins the book not by greeting the Galatian believers as he does in his other epistles, but by establishing his authority over them as one sent not by men, but by God, Himself. Although he politely extends grace and peace to them, (1:3) again unlike his other epistles, he doesn't share any blessing with them. He doesn't comment on his thankfulness for them, and there is no recording of his prayers on their behalf. Instead, he launches immediately into a fiery rebuke concerning their decision to stray from the faith and the dire consequences of that choice. Galatians Chapter 4, to me, is the apex of Paul's frustration with the Galatian believers and their willingness to forget the blessing of their salvation. Paul reprimands them because of their decision to return to what he refers to as "weak and worthless elemental things" which would once again enslave them. Where previously these young believers had rejoiced in the truth of the Gospel, as shared with them by Paul, now when the reality of life and its trials squeezed them, they had lost their sense of blessing. In modern vernacular, Paul was asking them, "What in the world has happened to your joy?"

At one point, the truth of the Gospel and their relationship with both God and Paul had been a source of joy to the Galatians. Now, according to Galatians 4, that truth had become an anathema to them and Paul had become their enemy. Because the Galatian believers had willfully forgotten that their joy came from the very truth of the Gospel that had changed their lives, their circumstances became like blinders, quenching their joy and robbing them of their settled security in Christ. Please don't misunderstand, the Apostle Paul was in no way trying to judge what the joy of the Galatian believers *looked like*. Instead, what he was addressing was the clearly apparent lack of joy in their lives.

Have you ever had a spiritual mountaintop experience? Think of how your kids are when they return from a spiritual summer camp trip. Often, they are overflowing with joy. They are excited about their walk with the Lord and full of ideas for how they are going to spend more time in the Word, memorize more Scripture, listen to more uplifting music, and give up those areas of life that are stumbling blocks. But, just how long does that spiritual high last? Inevitably, their excitement fades and old, comfortable habit patterns reestablish their dominance.

Just like our kids, the Galatians had experienced a spiritual high while Paul was with them. Regardless of how hard the truths that he taught, and regardless of the sacrifices that they would have to make in order to walk faithfully with Christ, they were eager to make those life changes. But now... Now Paul wasn't physically present with them and, the excitement of living with and learning from the apostle was being drowned out by contrary voices. Without the spiritual high of daily interactions with Paul, the Galatians had lost their sense of blessing. They had lost their clearness of conviction. Truly, it appeared that they had lost their joy!

There is no one-size-fits-all expression of joy, but when joy is missing, as it was in the lives of the Galatian believers, it leaves behind an unmistakable void that masks and misrepresents our God. Honestly, joyless believers stick out like a sore thumb. Joyless believers are like insect repellent. Instead of drawing others to their joy, they repel and drive away each and every person in their path.

Let's be really practical for a minute. In fact, if you'll

allow me to meddle, I want to ask you to consider yourself carefully. Like it or not, we women are the emotional hub of our homes. If we are agitated, our husband and children will be agitated. If we are scattered and unorganized, our entire home will feel out of control. And, most importantly, if we are lacking in joy, that lack of joy will quickly turn the sanctuary of our homes into a prison of joyless drudgery and religious obligations.

Please don't misunderstand me, joy doesn't always show itself as an exuberant expression of excitement. Remember, for the believer joy is that settled, secure contentment and recognition that because of our eternal salvation and the promises of God, we can entrust ourselves to the loving hand of our Father. Sometimes joy's greatest expression is found in the calm, consistent obedience of fulfilling our daily responsibilities with a thankful, joy-filled heart. Sometimes, the joy in our heart is externally silent, but that doesn't make it any less joy-filled. And sometimes, our joy bubbles over on the outside, drawing others into our circle of Christ-generated joyfulness!

I'm convinced that there are probably as many expressions of joy as there are different personalities among believers. I mentioned previously that I'm an introverted personality. (Some would even call me melancholy.) Although my heart is full of joy on a continual and daily basis, I would describe my joy as a *quiet* joy. I'm not overly excitable and I'm definitely, positively, absolutely NOT exuberant! It tires me out to even think of being exuberant! On the other side of the equation, one of the young women that I spend time discipling is a vibrant extrovert. When she speaks of the Lord, her eyes sparkle, and she just bubbles over with extravagant joy. Her joy is contagious, and our time together always lifts my spirits and encourages my heart. We're pretty much complete opposites; however, both of us are equally joyful. For both of us, our joy is a settled secure contentment and a recognition that because of our salvation, our days and lives are safe in the hands of our loving God. Thankfully, both of us are able to exhibit that joy in a manner that is true to who we are and respectful to God's unique design for each of our personalities.

How does joy manifest itself in your life? Are you an outward expresser? Do you burst into joyful song or trip over your own words as you talk to others about the goodness of your God? Or, are you sedately joyful, sharing your joy through handwritten notes or shared times of prayer? There is no one-size-fits-all manner of expressing and experiencing joy. I really want to encourage you not to look at anyone else's outward joy and despise or doubt your own expressions of joyful living!

I don't believe that God is worried about *how* we're expressing our joy, but rather, *are* we living a joy-filled Christian life? Having blinders on that keep us from seeing the joy that is set before us is serious business for the believer for three very important reasons. First, it robs God of the glory that He is due. Secondly, it clouds our hope and, therefore, our testimony as children of God. Finally, it hides Jesus and His salvation from the eyes of a watching world.

Matthew 5:1–16 teaches much about the necessity of living joyfully. Many of you will recognize this as the chapter of the Bible that contains the Beatitudes. As Jesus was teaching the multitudes, He laid out a comprehensive list of counter-intuitive truths. For example, when we're poor, we're actually rich in the kingdom; when we're gentle, we'll inherit the earth; when we're persecuted and men speak evil of us, we'll be blessed. Everything He taught was opposite of what the culture recognized as the normal way to succeed in life.

But consider carefully verse 12. After laying out all types of contrary-to-normal actions, Jesus ends His counter-intuitive commands with what might have been the hardest command of all. After reminding those following Him that they would face misunderstanding and judgment, He commanded them to "Rejoice." Are you like me? Is that command hard to swallow? When people are unkind to me–or even worse, when they are unkind to my husband or children–the last thing I want to do is rejoice! Grumble, retaliate, complain... Sure! But rejoice? That's a hard one! For now, tuck into the back of your mind that when you see rejoice, you should think *an outward expression of joy*.

In verse 16, our Lord went on to share the real reason for His counter-intuitive teaching. He concluded His instructions with this explanation: "Let your light shine before men in such a way that they may see your good works, and glorify you Father who is in heaven." There you have it. When we live counter to our culture and counter to our own nature, and when we rejoice as we're doing so, we bring glory to God. There is no greater purpose in heaven or on earth. God is honored through our glory-bearing joy.

Having spent a majority of my adult life living near the coast of New England, Jesus' use of a light set on a hill evokes strong images for me. The beautiful New England coastline is dotted with quaint lighthouses. Each of those lighthouses is unique in its configuration and outward exterior, but each of the lighthouses was constructed for the same practical purpose. They were never built simply to become an attractive tourist destination. No, the lighthouses were meant to guide both large and small ships safely to shore. The rocky New England coastline has some terrible fog, and lighthouses were a beacon of safety to those in the boats. Sometimes when the night was clear, the light from the lighthouse illuminated brightly. However, at other times when the fog rolled in, all that the sailors could see was the dimmest pinpoint of light.

Shining as lights is the same for us. Some Christians will shine vividly and their light will illuminate many. But, other Christians will shine softly. Their soft, undimming light will be the exact guidance back to the safety of the Lord that certain people will need. Living joyfully isn't about our voltage, but about our consistent commitment to shining for Jesus.

Whether exuberant or quiet, in the smallness of our homes or in our greater community, when it's easy or when it's hard, our purposeful choice to hang on to joy and to show forth that joy to others is essential. When we exhibit our joy through rejoicing, regardless of our circumstances, we will glorify our God, bring light to our testimonies, and magnify Christ before the unsaved. By contrast, when we choose to allow our circumstances to drive our emotions and block our joy, we will diminish God's glory and do harm to the cause of Christ.

The things of this life can never bring us permanent joy. Although they may thrill or satisfy for the moment, they are never a replacement for the Christ-focused joy that God desires His own to experience. There is no substitute for the joy we find in Christ!

Let me encourage you to spend time this week seeking God in prayer. Ask Him to constantly bring to remembrance this Biblical truth: *You can find joy in the settled security of your relationship with Him and His promise to bring good into your life.* Petition God for the strength and conviction to put-off the joy-squashing circumstances that seemingly threaten to rob you of the joy of your salvation, and to instead put-on the truth of Christ as found in the Word of God. In a later chapter, we'll spend time considering specific and practical ways to combat the enemies of our joy. However, for now, solidify this truth in your heart: Regardless of the enemy, God always wins the battle! Although we may wage war with circumstances and emotions, His victory is made sure and our joy is secure.

PERSONAL APPLICATION:

- What circumstances or situations seem to be threatening to rob you of your joy, today?

- Considering those difficult circumstances, what emotion or emotions are being exposed in your heart? (i.e. fear, doubt, bitterness, anger...)

- Using your Bible's concordance (or Google ☺) find at least two Scriptures that speak to each of the negative emotions that you are experiencing. Record those Scriptures below. Please write out the entire verse, not simply the reference. After you have written out each of the verses, choose one to memorize this week. Remember,

memorizing Scripture gives the Holy Spirit a tool
to use in your heart. Whether it's through
conviction, encouragement, or just calming
reassurance, God's Word, hidden in our hearts, is
the best weapon to combat those wrong thoughts
that assail us. (Psalm 119:11)

JOY IS A REALLY BIG DEAL

"The pursuit of true virtue includes the pursuit of the joy because joy is an essential component of true virtue. This is vastly different from saying, "Let's all be good because it will make us happy."

– John Piper

In Chapter One, we defined joy. We considered how the permanence of Christ-focused and God-given joy can never be replaced by circumstantial happiness. People, things, and situational successes only provide momentary pleasure. But what if we don't have either? What if we aren't particularly joyful but not just seeking happiness, either? What if we're just quietly doing our own thing and minding our own business? Isn't the same-old-same-old of a consistent life enough for us?

If life was just about us and our own personal well-being, perhaps just walking through our days with quiet stoicism would suffice. But life isn't just about us! Our lives are to be a living representation of our Savior, so it's important to see what the Scriptures have to say about the necessity of joy in the daily life of the believer.

Although joy–or a lack of joy–may seem to be an emotions-driven feeling, the truth is that joy is an act of obedience. In the same way that the Scriptures call us to obedience in matters of praying, serving, giving, and confessing, we are just as imperatively called to obedient joyful living. The Bible clearly commands us to be joyful, so that command alone should become the foundation for our decision to living joyful, Christ-honoring lives. For the believer, it's vital that our inward joy shows itself outwardly through rejoicing. In fact, as we'll discover over and over throughout the Scriptures, inward joy and outward rejoicing are intrinsically inter-related.

For me, Philippians 3:1 is one of the Scripture's clearest examples of the believers marching orders from God:

FINALLY, my brethren, rejoice in the Lord. To write the same things again is no trouble to me, and it is a safeguard for you.

ACTUALLY, Paul considered joy to be such an important topic that in the short epistle to the Philippian church, he returned to the topic twelve times. If you take the time to look up the following verses, you'll get a crystal- clear picture of Paul's heart concerning joy and its outward manifestation as shown through rejoicing: 1:4; 1:18; 1:25; 2:1; 2:17; 2:18; 2:28; 2:29; 3:1; 4:1; 4:10. WOW!

I'm not at all surprised that Paul thought it was so necessary to continually remind the Philippian believers to remember their joy. I don't, however, think he was writing to them as one who was disappointed in their forgetfulness.

Remember, Paul was just as human as we are. In fact, the Scriptures record that he had moments of discouragement, broken relationships, thwarted plans, and opportunity-altering imprisonments. I'm sure his reminder to the Philippians was a reminder to himself, as well. And, like Paul and like the Philippian believers, we need those reminders, too. What a sweet privilege we have to remind one another to rejoice. We'll learn in a later chapter about how to fulfill that responsibility to one another wisely. For now, please understand that as a *joy-bearer*, it is a tremendous privilege to become a *joy-sharer*!

Let's consider some more of Paul's teachings. From the moment that the Thessalonian believers heard and received the truth of the Gospel, they became the targets of hateful persecution. Both Jews and Greeks were enraged by these new Christians. In the book of I Thessalonians, Paul is writing to check on the welfare of these young believers and to encourage them to live triumphantly in spite of the bitter opposition. I Thessalonians 5:16 is one of the shortest, yet most commanding, verses in the Scriptures. To these persecuted young believers, Paul gave this simple, but compelling command ... "Rejoice always." Paul compassionately recognized the persecution that they were experiencing, yet he gave no caveat or exception to his command. Regardless of their trials or difficult circumstances, the Thessalonian believers had only one choice if they wanted to remain faithful to their God. *They would have to make the choice to rejoice.*

The word *rejoice* literally means *to show forth joy*. The Apostle Paul certainly wasn't encouraging the Thessalonian believers to attempt to manufacture some type of man-made outward joy as an escape from their trials. Instead, he was providing them with a practical action step to take in spite

of their trials. In the next two verses, Paul gave the Thessalonian believers a safe place to run with their crushing trials
and heartaches. Consider what he told them in I Thessalonians 5:17–18:

PRAY WITHOUT CEASING; *in everything give thanks; for this is
God's will for you in Christ Jesus.*

YES, the command to *rejoice always* would be a hard choice
to make in the midst of difficulties, but Paul knew that both
the obedience of rejoicing and the security found in
thankful prayer were the best medicine for the hurting,
fearful hearts of the Thessalonians. Today, Paul's admonition to the Thessalonians is also an admonition to us.
When circumstances are hard and trials threaten to overwhelm us, we will be helped in our journey by our obedient
choice to rejoice, followed by a full-on sprinting run to the
Lord with our thankful petitions. Again, it's counter-intuitive. Our flesh would have us wallow and self-protect, but
our gracious God, through the words of the apostle, has
given us the best antidote to the trials and worries that
assail us.

As we consider Paul's exhortations to both the Philippian and Thessalonian believers, it becomes very apparent
that joy is an ACTION. Although joy can be outwardly
expressed through feelings or emotions, it is first and foremost an attitude of the heart. That means that the *action* of
joy is only possible as we possess an *attitude* of joy. Joy is a
choice, and for every believer it is the choice to be obedient
to the Word of God. Joylessness, then, is the result of inac-
tion and disobedience. When it comes to clinging to our joy,

we must become active participants in our own spiritual growth, not passive children waiting to be urged unto joy.

It's true that sometimes the circumstances of life in which we find ourselves make glorifying God through our joyful living much more difficult. Remembering that joy is first and foremost an act of obedience will help us tremendously as we choose the daily discipline of glorifying God through our joy and rejoicing. I love what pastor and teacher, Clarence M. Keen had to say about joy in the midst of our circumstances:

CIRCUMSTANCES MAY NOT ALWAYS BE conducive to rejoicing, but look up and away to Calvary. Circumstances are the things about us, but our Lord sits in the heavens above us, and the Holy Spirit is within us. Rejoice!

AS IMPORTANT AS it is for us to choose joy daily through bringing our hearts and actions into obedience to the Lord, there's an even greater good that is accomplished by our joy-filled living. When we choose to acknowledge the gift of joy that was given us through and by our salvation, we bring glory to our God. I Corinthians 10:31 reminds us:

WHETHER, then, you eat or drink or whatever you do, do all to the glory of God.

ISN'T it interesting that Paul picks two of the most mundane activities of life and reminds us that even in the mundane, *we can and must bring glory to God.* Not a day goes by that I don't manage to eat several meals, if not more. (Whether I need to or not!) I think that what Paul is telling us is that if we can be focused on bringing glory to God in something that seems so simple and mundane–eating and drinking–we will be training ourselves to bring glory to God when it isn't so easy–in hardships and trials. The daily discipline of learning to practice joy in the little things of life will prepare us to win the battle and hold fast to joy when things are hard. When we can do that, our God will be glorified.

Even as I'm working on the final draft of this book, our nation is plunged into the craziness of the Covid-19 pandemic. Many men and women are losing their lives to the Coronavirus while at the same time our economy is being devasted by the closing of all non-essential businesses. Many are facing both the fear of illness, as well as the dread of long-term unemployment. America has never in her history faced a time such as this. So how should we, as Christians, approach these troubling times? It's very clear from the Scriptures that today, as in the early church, we are to rejoice and pray. Sadly, however, many Christians are finding themselves mired in the same gray bucket of worry that is entrapping the unsaved world. Why is that?

Frankly, this old axiom is still true today ... *We fight the way we train!* The success we maintain in stewarding our Biblical joy through any hardship is directly related to our pre-trial training. Have we been working out our spiritual muscles through time in the Word, prayer, Scripture memorization, serving others, true Biblical fellowship, and, most importantly, a daily striving to put-off the old man and put-on the new man? (Ephesians 4:22–24) Have we been intentionally training ourselves in preparation for the inevitable trials of life? Or, have we been busy pursuing our temporary happiness, and now we are caught off-guard and ill-prepared for spiritual success?

A couple of my children are excellent athletes. Each pre-season, like clockwork, they lay out an elaborate training plan to begin preparing for the upcoming season. Each off-season, like clockwork, their training plan gathers dust as other more exciting options fill their days. (And when girls entered the scene, training plans definitely became option-al!!) Honestly, neither of my boys will ever be professional athletes, so being lax in their preseason training isn't the end of the world. However, for us, failing to prepare spiritu-ally in our times of normalcy and mundane living can lead to tremendous spiritual failure when trials suddenly come upon us. If we want to glorify God and continue to exhibit His gift of joyful living to our families and friends, we're going to have to *bump up* those off-season spiritual work-outs. Regular spiritual training will build strong spiritual muscles and a consistent spiritual muscle memory, A consistent spiritual muscle memory is the only way we will be able to habitually choose joy, regardless of our circum-stances.

Perhaps I should explain what I mean by *spiritual muscle memory*. As you may have guessed already, I'm a pretty big sports fan. I've been a swimmer-mom, baseball-mom, soccer-mom, and cross-country-mom. Besides spending an inordinate amount of time travelling to sporting events and cheering on my athletes, I also love reading about what makes athletes successful. One of the most researched topics in sports training is the topic of predictable muscle memory. For athletes the more often they can complete an athletic task correctly and instinctively, the more successful they will be in their athletic endeavors.

For example, from the time that Tiger Woods was a

small boy, his father insisted that he practice swinging his golf club correctly. Over and over Tiger kept his head down, bent his knees, and made sure to follow through with his swing. Over, and over, and over again. According to athletic trainers, predictable muscle memory involves repeating the same motion or action eight to ten thousand times. At this point, I doubt that Tiger Woods can swing his club incorrectly. His muscles have built a predictable habit pattern that causes them to consistently perform with excellence.

So, it is with our spiritual muscles. If we only exercise our faith in times of trial, rather than building it during times of normalcy, we will never be confident that our faith can withstand hardships. If we only pray sporadically, rather than developing a persistent and consistent prayer life on a regular basis, our prayers will be ineffective. Honestly, we'll be left wondering if God even hears us.

If our joy is only evident when it's accompanied by circumstantial happiness, we'll flounder in joylessness when troublesome events or wounded relationships shatter our normalcy and routine. However, if our relationship with the Lord is thriving through faith-building and joy-filled growth, our spiritual muscles will be strong, and we will be able to trust those spiritual muscles to respond biblically, regardless of our circumstances. When it comes to building spiritual muscles and predictable spiritual muscle memory, we must *BULK UP!*

King David was a man, who faced trials, temptations, worries, and fears much like us. His beautiful heart-cries in the psalms provide a clear picture of how he learned to hand the enemies of his joy over to the Lord in prayer and praise. Because he learned to hand those joy-enemies over consistently, he was able to live a secure and joy-exhibiting life, in spite of hardships and betrayal. His words in Psalm

63:3–8 are a tremendous testimony that can give us hope and help as we face our own hardships:

Because Thy lovingkindness is better than life, My lips will praise Thee. So I will bless Thee as long as I live; I will lift up my hands in Thy name. My soul is satisfied as with marrow and fatness, And my mouth offers praises with joyful lips. When I remember Thee on my bed, I meditate on Thee in the night watches, For Thou hast been my help, And in the shadow of Thy wings I sing for joy. My soul clings to Thee; Thy right hand upholds me.

As David recalled God's power, glory, lovingkindness, and personal help, he was satisfied, and the result was heartfelt prayers of joy. His mouth rejoiced from a place of security under the watchful care of God.

Interestingly, it wasn't God's protection, provision, or blessing that caused the Psalmist to rejoice and glorify God. It was simply His name. God's name is who He is, and His name alone makes Him worthy of glory and praise. When we, like David, recognize how deeply God loves and cares for us, we'll eagerly find every opportunity to rejoice and praise Him for who He is and for what He has done for us.

Psalm 105:3–5 provides another example of David's joy in his relationship with the Lord. It's obvious from the exultant words of the Psalmist that as he glorified the Lord, his joy (gladness) was overflowing. That overflowing gladness didn't come from a once a week, or once a month, or an every-holiday season trip to see the Lord. Rather, it came from David's commitment to seeking the Lord continually. As he did so, he then was filled with remembrances of all that the Lord had done for him: God's wonders, (extraordinary or remarkable acts or achievements) His marvels, (something awe-inspiring or astounding) and His judgments (Divine sentence or decisions).

The daily decision to cultivate a habitually joyful heart will remind us that there is Someone bigger than we are to deal with the hard realities of life. God can and will work on our behalf. However, He won't force Himself into the role of rescuer. When we try to fix-it on our own, we are robbing Him of His role and rightful glory. Even more so, we are missing out on joy-filling opportunities to see God's wonders, marvels, and judgments at work in our very own lives.

Have you ever stopped to consider that everything, whether good or bad, that comes into your life has already passed through the *approval process* of God? Nothing catches Him by surprise! If we are facing a new or difficult situation, we can trust that our God has already seen it and determined that it will be profitable for our spiritual growth. In every circumstance of life, there are really two equal, but opposite, parts to the equation. Our part of the equation is our responsibility to glorify God. (I Corinthians 10:31) However, on the other side of each situation is the responsibility that belongs to God. His responsibility is to bring about good through—or sometimes in spite of—our circumstances. (Romans 8:28) It looks something like this:

EVERY CIRCUMSTANCE = Our good + God's glory
　　Our good = God's job
　　God's glory = Our job

. . .

HERE'S where we run into a problem ... We get all wrapped up trying to figure out the "our good" part of the equation. We *what if*, and *if only*, and *I've got this* trying to make situations and circumstances work out the way that we think is best. We use our limited experience to determine what will produce the most happiness in our lives. We've got to STOP IT! As my kids say to each other, "Stay in your lane, bro." We can never accurately determine what *good* will look like for us. Only God knows the answer to that question. In fact, sometimes what He determines as good, looks like just the opposite to us. But good is His job. He's got it! If we were half as worried about doing our job–that whole bringing God glory part–He'd be glorified and magnified, we'd be blessed, and the world would stand amazed.

It doesn't matter how hard, or confusing, or frustrating, or frightening the circumstance we face, it's God's responsibility, and His alone, to bring about the good that only He can produce from our trial. Our one and only responsibility is to bring Him glory by, through, and even in the midst of our situation. When we try to fill God's shoes, we are woefully inadequate. In the process of trying to usurp His role, all we do is cause ourselves more worry and rob God of the glory that is due Him.

Sometimes, we all just need a gentle reminder of the great and wonderful things that the Lord has done for us. We need to remember how He has shown Himself powerful on our behalf. Please take just a few minutes and make a list of 5 ways that you have seen the hand of God personally working on your behalf. On days that you are struggling to find joy in your heart, referring back to this list will be an encouragement to continue to glorify God while trusting Him to bring about the good you so desperately need.

. . .

1.

2.

3.

4.

5.

ALL THROUGHOUT THE PSALMS, the memory of God's goodness resulted in the psalmist being brought to praise. Always, his praise ultimately resulted in glory to God. As we remember God's goodness to us, we, too, will produce that end result of praise and glory to our God. When you need a little memory boost, turn to the Psalms and allow the Word of God to remind you of His faithful goodness. When we remember God's goodness, His glory will flow from our hearts and mouths.

Steve and I have visited hundreds of churches over the past 10 years. I must confess that sometimes the church members' *Christian Joy* just isn't very evident on their faces. I'm afraid that visitors to some of our churches see arms-folded, serious-faced saints, instead of joy-spilling redeemed sinners saved by grace. I love the little children's song, "I've Got the Joy in My Heart," but honestly, the message of the song really misses the mark. The chorus of the song repeats the same message over and over ... I've got joy, it's down in my heart, it makes me happy, and down in my heart is where it's going to stay! The verses go on to speak of the love of Jesus, peace that passes understanding and wonderful love of our Blessed Redeemer, but all in the context of keeping those amazing joy-producing truths safely stowed away down in our hearts.

Ladies, it is because of the love of Jesus, and the peace that passes understanding, and the wonderful love of our Blessed Redeemer that we have every reason to overflow with joy. That kind of joy just can't be contained! Rather than hiding that joy deep down in our hearts, where only we will receive the blessing of it, let's allow the precious joy of the Lord to course through our veins and affect our every thought, action, communication, and relationship.

Yes, joy must first transform our own hearts. But after our hearts have been changed, transformed, and filled with God-given joy, the outward expression of that joy through rejoicing is absolutely essential. As we magnify Christ through expressions of joyful living, He will use our joy as a tool in His transformation of the hearts of unbelievers! As His children, our life-long goal should be to become a *living* expression of joy. That *life* is the life of Christ in us, the hope of glory! (Colossians 1:27)

PERSONAL APPLICATION:

- There are so many mundane tasks that make up our daily responsibilities and to-do lists. Choose one of those tasks and record three ways that you can outwardly exhibit joy as you complete what seems to be just a simple chore. After recording

those three, practical action-steps, choose one to
put into practice this week.

- Spend some time in prayer this week and
  honestly ask the Lord to show you any
  circumstances in your life that are tempting you
  to usurp and take over His role. Write down what
  you learn through your prayer time. Afterwards,
  make a commitment that on a daily–maybe even
  hourly or minutely–basis, you will choose to
  hand that circumstance back to the Lord.
  Purpose to instead focus on bringing Him glory
  through your faithful trust, obedience, and joy.
- If you're wondering how to go about transferring
  the ownership of your hard circumstances to the
  Lord, read II Corinthians 10:5.

A SCRIPTURE that has been helpful to me as I learn to let go
of what isn't mine in order to hand those things back to God
is I Peter 5:7: *Casting all your anxiety on Him, because He cares
for you.* The word cast in that verse is literally like playing
Hot Potato. Remember as a child passing a hot potato from
person to person as quickly as possible so that you weren't
the one left holding the hot potato when the timer ran out?
(Actually, my generation played Time Bomb with a wind-up
bomb!) In the same way I threw that time bomb to the next
person as quickly as I could, God wants me to throw my
fears, cares, anxieties, worries, and troublesome situations
to Him. He's never caught unawares, and He never drops

what I throw to Him! That little mental picture has been a great reminder when trouble threatens to consume my thoughts. No matter the trouble, I can throw it away to my eagerly waiting Catcher.

- Finally, pick one of the verses that we studied this week and commit it to memory. Continue reviewing last week's verse. By the time we complete this study, you'll have a storehouse of verses to strengthen and encourage your heart!

4

THERE'S MORE TO JOY THAN MEETS
THE EYE

G od designed people to mimic what others believe and
value, what they choose, how they behave from their
earliest days. God's primary instruction to people—the
center of his will for humankind—is that they love him with the
full breadth of their hearts and teach their children to do the
same. When people believe God's Word,
value his character, and submit to his will, they will influence
others with whom they interact while sitting in their house
together, walking in the street, lying down and rising up, coming
in and out of the gates (Deuteronomy 6:7–9). What people
primarily love in their hearts shapes others under their influence.

– Jeremy Pierre

AS WE'VE LEARNED THUS FAR, joy is an act of obedience, and
our obedient joy has the end result of bringing glory to God.
But there are two other important reasons that joy is an
imperative in the life of the believer. Let's consider the

personal impact that joy has not only on us, but also on those with whom we have relationships.

Choosing joy will transform us. When we are transformed, we have the opportunity to influence transformational change in the world around us. Practically speaking, that means that our inward joy and outward rejoicing can produce positive, Christ-focused change in the lives of our family, friends, co-workers, and neighbors. What a privilege we have to show others what Christ has done in our lives as they witness our joy-filled response to trials.

In Isaiah 35:10, the prophet shows us the natural progression of joy in the transformation of a believer. First, we are changed inwardly, as seen in the *everlasting joy on the head of the ransomed of the Lord*. Then, after that inward change, the outward expression of our joy will be *gladness and shouting*. But Isaiah didn't just happen upon that everlasting joy; first, he experienced sorrow and sighing. Like us, his life wasn't easy, but the transforming joy of the Lord changed his attitude. Then he, in turn, took practical steps to change his circumstances.

When I read the book of Isaiah, there's no doubt in my mind that the prophet experienced the same emotions that we experience. He was a fellow-struggler who needed the joy of the Lord to walk through difficult days. When I am struggling to find joy in a trial or troubling situation, like Isaiah, I so often spend my days in sorrowful sighing. Sometimes, it feels as though I'm carrying a heavy boulder on my shoulders. Here, in Isaiah 35, the prophet gives us the antidote to that type of soul-exhausting struggle. We must return to the Lord with an obedient heart and then, we will be filled with God-given joy and gladness.

Just a side-note to consider: There are many times in the Scriptures that we see people who choose NOT to return to the Lord. God ultimately used that choice to bring about His own honor and glory. However, they also reaped the hard consequences of their decision not to return. For example, when Naomi and her husband Elimelech traveled to Moab and remained there, (Ruth 1:2) Naomi experienced nothing but grief and sorrow in her foreign home. In fact, when she finally did return to Bethlehem in Judah, Naomi had changed her name to Mara, which means bitter. It took the miraculous working of God on behalf of her and Ruth for Naomi to again recognize God's blessing and find joy.

In like manner, the historical context of the book of Esther indicates that Mordecai could have–and really should have–chosen to return to Jerusalem after the death of Nebuchadnezzar. However, he chose to remain behind in Susa in spite of both the prophets Isaiah and Jeremiah instructing the Israelites to return to the land of Palestine. (Isaiah 48:20; Jeremiah 50:8, 51:6) Although God used the horrible situation that arose against Israel to His glory, Esther, as Mordecai's charge, faced becoming part of a harem and the forced queen of an evil king. All because of the decision by Mordecai to NOT return to the land.

On a personal level, I've experience firsthand what it means to choose *not* to return to God. As a young engaged woman, I was deeply involved in the ministry of Young Life. I loved working with teenagers, and I couldn't even imagine not being involved as a Young Life leader. Older staff members were encouraging me to enter their training program after college and to become a Young Life staff member. At the same time, I was engaged to Steve, a Navy pilot who would be frequently moving from duty station to duty station. The two options just weren't compatible. Even as I prayed about the situation, I knew in my heart that without a doubt, God wanted me to marry Steve. But I wanted to be on Young Life Staff! It wasn't that I didn't love Steve; it was just that staff seemed so glamorous, and exciting, and rewarding, and besides, everyone said I was a natural! (Can you picture my much-inflated ego?)

Believe me when I tell you that I had absolutely NO PEACE until I put aside my desire for Young Life and committed fully to becoming Mrs. Steve Scheibner. At the time, I thought that I would never be involved in ministry again! I was only 22, *and the drama was real.* I never could have pictured the many ways that God would allow me to serve Him in the past 35 years! (Including a one-year stint on Young Life Staff–God's sense of humor!) But, God knew! And He gently walked alongside me as I returned to the security of His will for my life. Returning to God meant saying no to self and no to some of my less-than-humble desires. However, like Isaiah, once I returned, my sighing and sorrow fled and the end result was gladness and joy.

And just in case you wonder if refusing to return to the Lord will only affect you ... In 1998, Steve was preparing to graduate from seminary. He had begun his education with no particular ministry goal in mind, but during his time in seminary, the concept of church planting had become an exciting option to him. As he neared the end of his seminary training, Steve was faced with two alternatives. He could either begin the process of preparing to launch a new church plant, or he could take on a new role as the Commanding Officer of his reserve Navy Squadron. Years earlier, Steve had written a spiritual life objective that he utilized often to help him make wise spiritual decisions. His spiritual life objective said this: *To seek, trust, and glorify God through humble service and continual prayer, and to raise up qualified disciples as quickly as possible, so that someday, I might hear God say, "Well-done my good and faithful servant."*

Just reading that spiritual life objective makes it pretty obvious which of the two choices was the right choice for our future. There was nothing written there about leading tactical missions, directing squadron affairs, or administering detachments and deployments. There was, however, much about glorifying God, serving humbly, and training other followers of Christ. Easy choice, right? Wrong! Steve, like me with the decision about Young Life, really, really wanted to be a Commanding Officer. He had worked his way up through the officer ranks and longed for the title. Regardless of the counsel that his spiritual life objective and other wise Christian men offered, he was bound and determined to have his own way.

Sometimes, choosing not to return to God simply involves a quiet, inward personal heart-struggle between us and God. At other times, however, the importance of the decision causes God to take decisive action for our good and His glory. As Steve doggedly pursued his vocational goal, he began to experience what the Scripture refers to as the *opposition of God*. (Galatians 5:17) In one short 48-hour period, Steve went from being ranked as the #1 officer in the squadron, to a new rank as the bottom officer in the squadron. No reason, no explanation, just a drastic change in his standing. Next, he missed a physical training exercise because he volunteered to be the instructor on a student flight. When he landed from the flight, he was given a written reprimand to put in his official folder. He argued that he'd missed the physical training because he was doing the front office a favor, but his argument was to no avail. In a breathlessly short amount of time, God ripped away Steve's option of becoming a Commanding Officer.

I wish I could tell you that God's lesson for Steve affected only him, but those next few weeks were an extremely difficult time period for our family. Steve is a verbal processor, and we all listened to him recount his indignation, unhappiness, and bitter disappointment over and over again. He was angry and unhappy, and that anger and unhappiness spilled over to the entire family.

At the same time that all of this was happening with the Navy, friends from Northern New England wrote asking Steve to consider planting a church in their community. The opportunity was exactly what he'd been talking about doing before the Navy position was extended to him. It was so obvious–even to Steve– what God was trying to bring about in his life. However, it was still a time-consuming process of submission and returning to God. His reluctant return caused turmoil for the whole family. Steve would tell you that God took him behind the woodshed for a good spanking, but those of us who loved him and watched him struggle through that discipline process were just as affected by the experience.

When we stubbornly refuse to submit and return to the Lord, our decision to disobey will squelch our joy and everyone we love will be affected. There is no such thing as a Lone Ranger Christian! One Christian's willful choices can have a devastating effect in the home, the church, and for the cause of Christ. But when we choose to submit and return to the Lord, everyone in our circle will be blessed right along with us. So many times, returning to the Lord means giving up what is good and permissible and replacing that thing with what is best and marvelous in the eyes of God. There is no regret in returning to the Lord.

Often, we can actually see the effect of our choice to return to God in the lives of those who walk alongside us. As we are blessed by God, others receive His blessing, as well. However, do you realize that there is also an unseen audi-

ence that is thrilled by our return? The angels, who can
never personally enjoy our status as sons of God, are filled
with joy at our return to the Lord. In the book of Luke, the
words of Jesus tell of the angels' joy:

IN THE SAME WAY, *I tell you, there is joy in the presence of the*
angels of God over one sinner who repents. –Luke 15:10

I TELL *you that in the same way, there will be more joy in heaven*
over one sinner who repents, than over ninety-nine righteous
persons who need no repentance. –Luke 15:7

GUESS WHAT ... it isn't only the unsaved who are sinners!
When we refuse to return to the Lord, we are smack dab in
the same *sinner* category as the unsaved, and we must
repent. Sometimes, returning to the Lord may be embarrassing, or humbling, or just downright hard, but remember,
we have an unseen audience that is filled with joy over our
return. The angels rejoice in heaven while at the same time
we are filled with God-given joy and gladness here on earth.

Happiness or a lack of happiness isn't–because of its
circumstantial nature– very reliable as an indicator of our
heart condition. However, a consistent lack of joy in our
daily lives oftentimes is a good barometer of our spiritual
health. If you find yourself dragging through the day with
no joy, spend some time carefully evaluating your personal
relationship with the Lord. Perhaps there are areas of your
spiritual life where it's going to be necessary for you to
return to the Lord in order to restore your joy.

Remember, joy isn't circumstantial; it's relationship-driven. If joy is missing, we must consider what's missing in relationship. Are we spending time in the Word getting to know our Lord better? Are we praying faithfully and pausing to reflect on God's answers to our prayers? Are we hiding His Word in our hearts, spending time with like-minded sisters in Christ, and serving others with an eager heart? Do we long to change in order to be more like Christ, and are we taking positive action to bring those changes about? The answers to these questions can help us to evaluate ourselves honestly when joy seems to be lacking in our lives.

The antidote to our sorrow and sighing, just as it was an antidote for the Old Testament saints and early church believers, is to return to the Lord. Anything that replaces the obedient response of joy in our hearts is a wandering from God! When we purposefully return to God, He will provide us with everlasting joy, (an inward transformation) that will lead to glad rejoicing (an outward expression).

Before we finish this chapter, let's consider one final but vitally important reason that joy is so essential in the life of God's people. When we are filled with joy and that joy is outwardly shown through our purposeful rejoicing, joy becomes an effective tool that is both evangelistic and missional.

Do you want to reach others for the cause of Christ? Does your heart ache for your friends, family, co-workers, and neighbors who are lost without hope of eternity? Do you want to be faithful as a minister of the Gospel?

BE JOYFUL!!!

. . .

PURSUING JOY IS NOT SELFISH! In fact, to pursue joy with your whole life is to honor the One who gave you that life. Unlike pursuing happiness, pursuing joy will always and eternally end in our personal ownership of joy. When joy becomes our own personal possession, we'll be able to freely and gladly share that joy with others.

Although Jim Berg and John Piper write and speak from two very different eschatological perspectives, they whole-heartedly agree on the Christian's freedom, or more actually obligation, to pursue joy. Consider what both of these Godly men have to say on the topic:

"EVERY TRIAL that ever burdened a mortal man, every temptation that ever stormed a human heart, and every blessing that ever delighted a needy soul have been skillfully designed by the Creator for one purpose: to draw men to Himself. Nothing else ultimately matter to God, and nothing else ultimately satisfies His creatures. God created man to be most satisfied, most joyful, and most useful when there is an ongoing, dependent, obedient, life-giving relationship with His Creator... The kind of relationship He has in mind for us will mean that both the Creator and the creature find their greatest joy in the joy of the other."—Jim Berg

"GOD IS NOT WORSHIPED where He is not treasured and enjoyed. Praise is not an alternative to joy, but the expression of joy. Not to enjoy God is to dishonor Him. To say to Him that something else satisfies you more is the opposite of worship. It is sacrilege... In communicating Himself to His creatures' hearts, and in their rejoicing and delighting in, and enjoying, the manifestations which He makes of Himself, God is glorified not only by His glory's being seen, but by its being rejoiced in. I must pursue joy *in God if I am to glorify Him as the surpassingly valuable Reality in the universe. Joy is not a mere option alongside worship. It is an essential component of worship.* —John Piper

PURSUING, chasing, or snatching joy is one of our greatest responsibilities. As we faithfully carry out that responsibility, we will gain a precious gift. Like the pearl of great price from Matthew 13:45–46, joy is worth selling all that we own and abandoning all that we claim as ours in order to pursue, find, and possess that great and wonderful gift of God ... Eternal and Everlasting Joy.

Because we live in a sin-stained and fallen world, pursuing joy is always going to be a battle. It is naïve to think that we can somehow get to a point when we will no longer face troubles and trials. However, we can become well-trained in the habitual discipline of pursuing joy *in spite* of those very troubles and trials. As we consistently and faithfully force our wayward hearts into the obedience of joy, our hard work will glean the eternal reward of inward joy for ourselves and transformational change in the lives of others. When men can see Christ firsthand through His lovingkindness towards us, they will be drawn to the Savior themselves.

In a later chapter, we'll spend time investigating and exposing those things that can trip us up in our efforts to live joy-filled and God-honoring lives. Learning to recognize our enemies will help us be prepared to do battle against those troublesome foes of our soul. For now, let's chew on these truths about the *why* behind the importance of joy by putting some personal applications into action.

Personal Application:

- Choose one of the four reasons why joy is so important and make a list of 5 practical action steps you can incorporate to ensure that you are placing the proper importance on that reason.

- Consider the ways that you already intentionally internalize joy. Record them below. Make a complementary list of ways that you can externally exhibit that internal joy to your family and friends.

- Finally, choose one of the verses from this week's study and commit it to memory. Don't forget to continue reviewing those verses that you have already memorized. ☺

THE UNMISTAKABLE CHARACTER OF JOY

"Mama's abounding joy of living carried our family and congregation through many such crises. We learned that the joy of the Lord was our strength. Proverbs 15:15 belonged to Mama: 'He that is of a merry heart hath a continual feast.' The immigrants shared their sense of humor as well as their joys and sorrows."–Margaret Jensen

It's one thing to know that we can have eternal joy. It's important to understand that the stewardship of that joy is a matter of obedience and responsibility. But just as importantly, we need to know exactly what God's Word says about joy. It's virtually impossible to steward something we don't understand, and it's dangerous to define joy on our own terms.

I'm not sure who first taught me about the word *JOY*, but I do know that early in my Christian life I was introduced to the concept that JOY stood for Jesus, Others, and You. Now although that's a splendid little acronym, I think it's an inaccurate concept. There's far too much emphasis on our role in the action of joy. If I were to make JOY an acronym, (Which of course, I must ... 'cause Christians love acronyms!) I would change the focus. My acronym would look like this:

J ... Jesus

O ...Our Heavenly Father

Y ... Your Comforter, the Holy Spirit

You see, we don't produce joy by our actions, or service, or self-care... God does! Joy is based solely on our joyful Triune God. Every part of joy starts and ends with God.

The Word of God tells us that joy came from God. It was created in the character of God. Joy came to earth through the birth of Jesus Christ. In fact, the word *Gospel* literally means *Message bringing joy*. Luke Chapter 2 recounts the birth of the Lord Jesus Christ. In verses 10–11, an angel appears to the shepherds bringing them *good news of great joy*. Think about that for just a moment. The joy that the angels brought was not because of the good news, but because of the child. Joy is found in the person and character of Jesus.

The message of the Gospel, although it convicts the sinner's heart and affirms the devastating truth concerning our eternal separation from God, is not meant to be communicated as a message of condemnation. Rather, the New Testament intention of the Gospel is that the life, death, and resurrection of Christ would be communicated as a message of great joy. To hear the Gospel is to hear the beautiful message of joy Incarnate.

Quite frankly, it's hard to communicate joy when circumstances are difficult. On our own and in our own strength, we just can't do it! If we want to be effective reflections of Gospel joy, we must find our strength and power to live and witness through the Holy Spirit. In the same way that Jesus came to earth bearing a message of joy, we know that the Holy Spirit, as the third person of the Godhead, is also a messenger of that same joyful Gospel. As we allow the Holy Spirit to guide and direct our lives, regardless of the harsh realities of life, we will become channels of that same Christ-like, Holy-Spirit imitating joy.

But how do we allow the Spirit to guide and direct us? At this point you may be thinking, "Sure Megan, but what does that *look like*?" Although there are hundreds, maybe even millions, of ways to submit ourselves to the Spirit, please allow me to offer just three suggestions as we seek to understand and experience the joyful life that the Spirit offers to us.

One of the most powerful avenues for experiencing the joy of the Holy Spirit is through frequent, consistent, and persistent prayer. Too often, prayer is our last resort. We turn to prayer when we're at the end of our rope. Instead, prayer must become the first place that we run to find help and hope. It's mind-boggling to me that God doesn't just allow us to pray ... He's eager to have us come to Him with our many needs. According to Proverbs 15:8, our prayers actually bring pleasure to our God.

Prayer isn't a second-best replacement for action. Rather, prayer is what prepares us to act. We can ask God to make joy *real* to our hearts. Knowing that God doesn't withhold any good thing from those who are His, we can be confident that His desire is that we would revel in His gift of joy. James 4:3 emphatically states:

You ask and do not receive, because you ask with wrong motives, so that you may spend it on your pleasures.

SEEKING to discover and appropriate our inheritance of joy is never about simply seeking relief for our problems. It isn't a quick fix for trials and hardships. Seeking to take ownership of our joy is always the path to a life of Christ-magnifying transparency. When we are filled to over-flowing with God-given and Christ-honoring joy, we will become those transparent believers who represent their Lord well. Transparency makes it possible for people to see less of us and more of the joy-producing Christ Who dwells within us. Trust me, if you see too much of Megan, you'll miss the beauty of Christ! My greatest desire is to become so personally invisible that when others see me, they actually see Jesus.

The second way to experience the joy that the Holy Spirit produces in our lives is through eager obedience. When we act quickly and completely, without question or complaint, in order to obey even the smallest direction of the Spirit, our obedience will produce joy. Disobedience is contrary to joyful living! It's so obvious in the lives of our children, isn't it? When they are choosing to disobey, although they may be enjoying the fleeting pleasures of sin in that moment, (Hebrews 11:25) they have no joy in their broken relationship with us. It's the same with us ... We grownups are just a tad more subtle. Delayed obedience or full-on disobedience to the Spirit will block the joy that God intends for us to experience. Disobedience causes distance in our relationship with the Lord.

The third way that we can experience joy is through serving others. Psalm 100 is one of the most joy-filled Psalms in all of the Scriptures. In the midst of the psalmist extolling God's goodness, lovingkindness, and faithfulness, he enjoins the people to service. That service, according to the psalmist, will bring about joyful shouting and singing. When we can be the physical hands of Jesus in service to others, the promised return blessing in our lives is joy. In the same way that prayer is too often our last resort, serving others too often becomes something we only do if it fits in our schedule and calendar. Joyfully serving the Lord isn't optional for believers who desire to walk in obedience and joyful relationship with their God.

Another truth that the Bible teaches about joy is that joy is a gift only for the believer. The unsaved can never experience the indwelling, eternal joy that is received through salvation. They do not have the promise that God has a plan for good for them. In fact, the only promise they can claim is the promise of eternal destruction, unless they repent and turn to the Lord.

Psalm 68 provides a stark contrast between the freedom of the righteous to rejoice in their God and the imprisonment of the wicked because of their separation from God. Verses 3–4 teach us how the righteous rejoice:

BUT LET *the righteous be glad; let them exult before God, Yes, let them rejoice with gladness. Sing to God, sing praises to His name; Lift up a song for Him who rides through the deserts, Whose name is the Lord, and exult before Him.*

ISN'T that quite a picture of the joy that results from the relationship that the righteous man enjoys with the Lord? Freedom from sin and a clean-hearted standing before a holy God provides the righteous with gladness. From that gladness, he pours forth in rejoicing. The righteous man's position before God causes gladness and rejoicing to walk hand-in-hand.

By contrast, the dwelling of the rebellious is a parched land. (vs. 6) That condition is as true for the rebellious of today as it was for the rebellious in the time of the Psalmist. Although sometimes it seems as though everything goes right for our unsaved friends ... they have big homes, fancy cars, Pinterest perfect lives ... the Scriptures makes it clear that they are, in fact, on the road to eternal destruction. (Psalm 73:18–20) The unsaved can neither win, nor work, their way to heaven. Our righteousness, attained through our salvation, gives us a positional title as sons of God. Because of that title, we have the freedom to rejoice and be glad before our God. No matter how much temporal success and worldly riches the unsaved attain, those things will never be as valuable as the peace and joy that is promised to those who belong to God.

Our joy isn't a finite object. It isn't that we're given joy once, and that initial gift is as much joy as we can ever expect to attain. Rather, the Scripture assures us that our joy can, and should, increase as we grow in our personal relationship with Christ. The prophet Jeremiah shows one of the ways that we can increase our joy. Jeremiah 15:16 paints an interesting picture of the impact of God's Word in the life of the believer.

THY WORDS WERE FOUND and I ate them, And the words became for me a joy and the delight of my heart.

THERE ARE several important things to notice in this one short verse. First, the Word of the Lord can be found! Our

God isn't hiding Himself from us. His desire is that we would know Him intimately, and the primary way we build that intimacy is through focused time in His Word.

However, Jeremiah didn't simply find the Word. In fact, as the verse states, he *ate* those words. The words weren't something that Jeremiah had a casual relationship with and admired from afar. No, he actually internalized the words. When the Lord's words became a part of him, those words then became his joy and delight. If we simply treat the Word as a casual acquaintance, it can never have that type of impact on our lives. On the other hand, when we approach God's words with a heart intent on change and growth, His words will become a part of our spiritual DNA.

There are really three aspects to our interaction with the Word of God if we want that Word to become our joy and delight. First, we must come to the Word with eager expectation. Eager expectation of what the Word is going to accomplish in our lives will prepare our hearts to be challenged and changed. If we simply approach the Word as an academic exercise or rote check-in-the-block matter of religious obedience, we run the risk of missing out on all that God has for us. Eager expectancy means that we will be ready to hear what God wants us to hear—whether it's encouragement, conviction, a direction to move, or the support we need to be still and wait. Eagerness is different than willingness when it comes to our interactions with the Word. I picture eagerness as being poised on the edge of my chair and ready to move at the slightest command of God. Willingness, on the other hand, is more like lounging on the couch and recognizing that I should get up ... just not right now. The more eagerly we approach the Word, the more quickly we'll see growth and change in our lives.

I think we all go through periods when our time in the

Word seems to be unfruitful. Perhaps, we are reading the Word daily, but what we read doesn't seem to be impacting our lives. Let me encourage you to continue on faithfully. Approach your time in the Word with a prayerful heart, asking God to reveal the necessary changes you must make in order to grow in Christlikeness. Focus your mind and heart on what you are reading. The beauty of spending time in the Word is that it builds a hunger to linger longer. As we internalize the truths we are mining from the Word of God, we will build an appetite for more truth.

I think of this concept as being the opposite of Thanksgiving dinner. Think about how you feel after consuming a Thanksgiving meal. Although we love the turkey, and stuffing, and mashed potatoes, and green bean casserole, and cranberry sauce, after we've eaten all of that, we can hardly manage to stagger to our couch. (And don't forget the apple pie; there has to be apple pie!) But the Word of God doesn't operate like that. The more time we spend in the Scriptures, the more time we will desire to spend there. It's another counter-intuitive Biblical truth. God's Word builds a hunger for more of God's Word.

The second aspect of our approach to the Word is a commitment to active obedience. Every day when I spend time in the Word, I try to remember to ask myself the question, "According to what I read today, how would God have me change to become more like His Son?" That little question keeps me focused. The Bible is a book of change, (Ephesians 4:22–24) but not just change for the sake of change. I want any change in my life to be Biblical change that conforms me to the image of Christ. More often than I'd like to admit, I recognize a needed area of change, I make a plan, (Or in my case, a list ... I Love Lists!) but I never take the necessary steps to bring about the change that God requires.

Making a commitment to actively obey the Word means that I will take purposeful and timely steps to follow the leading of God through His Word and the enablement of the Holy Spirit.

The final aspect of the Word becoming our joy and delight requires practicing steadfast stewardship. Steadfast stewardship surfaces in two different aspects of our relationship to the Word. After we have internalized what God is teaching us and taken practical steps to put that teaching into action, we must remain faithful to our new knowledge and practices. The New International Version translates Philippians 3:16 like this:

ONLY LIVE up to what you have already attained.

THAT VERSE TELLS me that God knows that we are forgetful believers! We need to be reminded that our active obedience isn't a once and done occasion. We don't have the luxury to *try on* the necessary changes that God reveals to us, only to return to our old habit patterns and sinful appetites. It's easy to become what I refer to as *change-addicts*. We get so excited about the next area of growth and change in our lives that we neglect to be faithful to the last area of change. In some sense, we begin to look like the double-minded man who was tossed to and fro as recorded in James Chapter 1. Instead, we are to be, as Philippians 3 reminds us:

... FORGETTING what lies behind and reaching forward to what lies ahead, I press on toward the goal for the prize of the upward call of God in Christ Jesus.

. . .

OLD HABITS DIE HARD; that's why we need to practice steadfast stewardship in order to keep those old habits tightly
nailed in the coffin of permanent change!

Steadfast stewardship also applies as we share the Word
of God with others. Being transparent about the changes
that God is bringing about in our lives will be an encouragement to others. As well, it will provide accountability for us.
There's nothing quite like sharing an area of growth and
change that you're trying to incorporate into your life and
having one of your children point out that you just failed in
that area, again. True friends will offer us that same type of
accountability-focused encouragement. (Only more gently
than our kids!) Sometimes it's humbling and sometimes it's
embarrassing, but accountability will help us on the road to
true growth and change. As we already discovered, Biblical
growth and change will provide a rich environment for
God's Word to become our joy and delight.

Delight is an interesting word. It means extreme satisfaction. Are you extremely satisfied with the Word of God? Or,
is the Word an interruption in your day? Is conviction for
needed change a gift or an intrusion? God wants His Word
to become for us a life-changing source of joy and delight.

I'm not exaggerating at all when I say that there is
nothing more precious to me than my Bible. When we are
on the road speaking, I always carry my travel Bible because
I don't want to take a chance on leaving my *good* Bible
behind in a hotel or conference room. (Trust me, I've lost
more than a few notebooks, sweaters, and coffee mugs that
way!) When I leave for our conferences, I make sure that
whoever is staying home knows where my Bible is located
and can grab it if the house catches on fire. Does that seem

extreme? Honestly, I don't think so. I've had my same Bible since 1993, and it truly is an invaluable record and reminder of my spiritual life. That Bible reminds me of who I was and, perhaps more importantly, the changes that God has produced in my life over these many years.

The more our Bibles become our primary tool for making wise choices in this daily life, the more we will find joy and delight in its pages. For years, I have underlined and dated passages in my Bible that have been used by God to prompt growth and change in my life. It's both reassuring and oftentimes convicting to revisit those underlined passages. Sometimes I read the passage, look at the date, and can thank God that whatever change He prompted previously is now a permanent part of my life. Unfortunately, other times I consider the dated, underlined passage and must repent and seek the Lord's forgiveness because although I instituted change at the time of the dating, I've now allowed myself to *forget* what the Lord had asked me to change. James 1:22–25 makes it clear that my *forgetfulness* keeps me from being blessed by the Lord.

BUT PROVE yourselves doers of the word, and not merely hearers who delude themselves. For if anyone is a hearer of the word and not a doer, he is like a man who looks at his natural face in a mirror; for once he has looked at himself and gone away, he has immediately forgotten what kind of person he was. But one who looks intently at the perfect law, the law of liberty, and abides by it, not having become a forgetful hearer but an effectual doer; this man shall be blessed in what he does.

. . .

I WANT to be a faithful *abider* who purposefully changes those unprofitable areas of my life that the Word exposes. Will you join me and make a commitment that you will approach the Word with eager expectancy, receive God's instruction with an attitude of active obedience, and faithfully continue to practice the changes He prompts in your life through steadfast stewardship? If we will allow the Word to transform, mold, and minister to our lives in such a way, that Word truly will become a joy and delight to us.

Before we conclude this chapter, let's consider one more very important truth that the Word of God teaches about our joy. According to the Scriptures, the joy that we experience here on earth is nothing compared to the immeasurable, incomparable joy that we will experience in the presence of Jesus. As I Corinthians 2:9 promises, *"eye has not seen and ear has not that heard ... all that God has prepared for those who love Him."* I can't wait!

Unimaginable joy was purchased for us by our Lord Jesus Christ as He died on the cross for our sins and was raised on the third day. Luke 42 recounts the events of the crucifixion of our Lord. I'm amazed that in the midst of such suffering and sorrow, Jesus took the time to reassure the thief on the cross beside him that *Today you shall be with me in Paradise.* What compassion in the thief's greatest moment of need. In one short statement, Christ told the thief three vitally important truths. First, He told him where they were going ... Paradise. Secondly, He told him when they would arrive ... today. And finally, and most importantly, He assured the thief of His presence there with him. What a wonderful promise, which was echoed by the Apostle Paul when he said:

. . .

To BE *absent from the body is to be present with the Lord.* —II *Corinthians 5:8*

JOY IS FOUND in the person of Jesus and how sweet will be our joy when we are safely in His presence for eternity. And, how frightening the future is for our unsaved friends and family. Proverbs 10:28 contrasts the difference between those futures.

THE HOPE *of the righteous is gladness, but the expectation of the wicked perishes.*

OUR FUTURE HOPE, because of our positional relationship with Christ, is gladness. Consider these synonyms for the word gladness: delight, blitheness, glee, cheer, hilarity, pleasure, mirth, and of course, joy. Can you even imagine how amazing heaven will be because gladness is the response of all who dwell there? How can we help but long for such a heaven with eager anticipation?

I'm so thankful that I can't *mess it up*! God promises that my eternal home will be with Christ, regardless of how joyful I feel in the moment, I can't lose my entrance to heaven. It is secured not by anything that I have done, but solely because of the substitutionary death of my Lord. In fact, even though I fail so often, the Scripture makes it clear that Christ alone will keep me from stumbling completely. Consider these promises in Jude 1:24–5:

Now to Him who is able to keep you from stumbling, and make you stand in the presence of His glory blameless with great joy, to the only God our Savior, through Jesus Christ our Lord, be glory, majesty, dominion and authority, before all time and now and forever. Amen.

WHAT A POWERFUL PROMISE from the half-brother of Jesus. Jude had vehemently denied the deity of Christ prior to the resurrection. Now, he refused to be known by his familial relationship with Jesus. Instead, Jude's only desire was to live and be known as the bondservant of Christ Jesus his Lord. If anyone had reason to be overwhelmed with thankfulness for the promise of an eternity with Christ, it was Jude. After denying as Lord the One whom he considered to simply be his half-brother, Jude was wonderfully given the redemptive opportunity to stand in Christ's presence forever.

Ponder the words of this humble half-brother of Christ. According to Jude, not only does Christ keep us from stumbling, but He makes us stand in His presence blamelessly and joyfully. What a tremendous and undeserved promise for Jude, and what an equally tremendous and undeserved promise for us. How can we be anything but joyful as we consider all that our Savior has provided for us?

PERSONAL APPLICATION:

- Can you remember a specific time that you chose obedience simply because of your deep love for the Lord? In a few sentences, describe both the choice that you made and the outcome of your choice. Consider carefully the spiritual fruit that blossomed because of your obedience to Christ.

- Is there some area of obedient change that you know needs to happen in order for you to honor God? Write down any change that needs to happen and the action steps necessary to bring that change about.

- Choose a memory verse for this week. Continue reviewing all of the past week's verses. Why not ask a friend or one of your children to quiz you this week?

OBEDIENCE: IT ISN'T JUST FOR KIDS

Too many Christians obey God only because of pressure on the outside, and not power on the inside ... We tend to please men, and to obey God only when others are watching. But when you surrender to the power of God within you, then obedience becomes a delight and not a battle. –Warren Weirsbe

I f you're anything like me, enforcing your children's obedience just isn't the highlight of your parenting day. Repeating the same instructions over and over and bringing about the necessary consequences when those oh-so-clearly-communicated instructions aren't obeyed is tiring at best and, at other times, just downright infuriating. If I had my choice, we'd just focus on the *good stuff*. We'd spend time reading books together, playing games, laughing, singing ... All the fun parts of parenting. So why do we keep doing it? Why do we continue to insist on obedience?

Honestly, that's an easy question to answer. We, as the parent, know that learning to obey now will help our children to be successful in their transition to young adulthood. We press on, always praying that as our children learn obedience to us, they will be learning the important heart attitudes that will make obedience to the Lord easier for them. I want my kids to recognize that it is a tremendous privilege to obey the God of the universe. The unsaved cannot enjoy that same privilege. They are, by nature, children of wrath and their natural obedience is to the ruler of this world. How sad!

As important as it is for our kids to realize their privileged position of obedience, it's just as important for us to realize the same thing. And just like we love to reward our children's obedience; God loves to reward ours. God isn't some sort of heavenly taskmaster who demands obedience and wields His authority with an iron fist. Instead, He is a gentle Father who loves to reward obedience. So often, that reward comes in the form of renewed or increased joy. I love what Elizabeth Elliot said about the ultimate purpose and outcome of our obedience:

GOD WILL NEVER DISAPPOINT US. *He loves us and has only one purpose for us: holiness, which in His kingdom equals joy.*

OUR OBEDIENCE ISN'T first and foremost for the purpose of making us joyful. Joy is the beautiful by-product of a life poured out in the pursuit of holiness (I Peter 1:16). Obedience, then, is our act of submission to our holy God as we seek to become more like Him. The joy that follows is His gift to us. A gift that strengthens and cheers us on our journey toward holiness.

May I encourage you to make your obedience-journey

truly yours alone? I'm afraid that our obedience is too often tempered by our horizontal relationships. In other words, we try to conform our obedience with what everyone else is doing. When this happens, Christianity risks becoming just another cookie-cutter religion, rather than an individual, Holy-Spirit prompted walk of obedience. Consider what Jerry Bridges says about this conformity of obedience in his wonderful book, *The Discipline of Grace*:

WE PRESS *the accelerator pedal of obedience until we have brought our behavior up to a certain level or "speed." The level of obedience is most often determined by the behavior standard of other Christians around us. We don't want to lag behind them because we want to be as spiritual as they are. At the same time, we're not eager to forge ahead of them because we wouldn't want to be different. We want to just comfortably blend in with the level of obedience of those around us.*

As A MOM, I absolutely hate when I see my children simply obeying certain rules just because everyone else obeys them. I want them to develop their own convictions. I want them to begin to understand what it means to hear the still small voice of the Lord and to act on that voice in obedience for themselves. I want their walk with the Lord to be undeniably theirs!

However, it isn't just kids that are guilty of this type of peer-focused obedience. We are just as prone to base the worthiness of our obedience on its conformity to the obedience of our circle of Christian friends. God deals with each and every one of us in unique ways. He demands obedience from me in areas that may never be demanded of you. And vice versa. As we move forward in this study and examine the obedience that cultivates and protects our joy, please, please, please focus on your own personal obedience.

In the next four chapters, we're going to examine some specific acts of obedience that the Scriptures promise will bring joy to our hearts. It's so important to know *what* we need to obey. Just because our parents lived a particular way, or our Christian friends consider something important, or our church has certain standards doesn't necessarily mean that what they obey is what we are to obey. I love how the Apostle Paul described the Berean believers. He said that they were a people who *examined the Scriptures daily, to see whether these things were so.* (Acts 17:11) Unless we search the Scriptures and base our obedience on Biblical truth and instruction, we are simply spinning our wheels and won't make any spiritual progress. Let's dig into the Scriptures and discover some areas of obedience that God promises will produce the spiritual fruit of joy.

Perhaps it goes without saying, but when we follow the Word of God, the end result will be joy. As we saw in an earlier chapter, *following* the Word is different than just *reading* the Word. Following the word requires a heart that is intent on obedience and change. These next few chapters are going to be pretty Scripture intensive, (Because let's face it ... We all need more of what God says and less of Megan.) so get your Bibles ready.

Let's begin by considering Psalm 119:14–16:

I HAVE REJOICED in the way of Thy testimonies, As much as in all riches. I will meditate on Thy precepts, And regard Thy ways. I shall delight in Thy statutes; I shall not forget Thy word.

. . .

REMEMBER, rejoicing is the outward manifestation of an inner heart attitude of joy. With that in mind, Psalm 119 presents some specific actions that the rejoicing believer can take in order to joyfully follow the Word. With rejoicing as the end goal, the believer must meditate, regard, delight, and never forget God's Word. As we study each of these actions individually, I believe we'll find some specific help in our journey of following God's Word.

The Psalmist begins by speaking of how he meditates on God's precepts. Precepts aren't just the specific laws that we find in the Scriptures, but instead the word *precept* encompasses God's actions and implied, not explicitly spoken, commands. One of the predictable results of spending time in fellowship with the Lord is a softening of the believer's heart. As our heart are softened, we will become more able to recognize those things that are of importance to God. Once we are able to recognize the actions and attitudes that are dear to God's heart, we can begin to obediently choose those actions and attitudes for ourselves.

Meditating on the Word is nothing like the world's definition of meditating. Instead of emptying our minds and just *being*, we must fill our minds with the Word of God and allow His Word to *mold and shape* us. That's one reason that it's so helpful to start our day in the Word. When we begin our day by reading the Scriptures, we will glean Biblical truth to meditate upon as we go throughout our day. Meditation on the Word, when coupled with an obedient response to the Word, will bring about growth and change as it increases our joy.

What does it *look like* to regard God's ways? The word regard is really synonymous with the word consider. As we consider God's ways, we will become more and more aware that He is God and we are not. It's so easy to begin to think of God as possessing the same character and attributes as us. Nothing could be further from the truth. The prophet Isaiah brings a timely reminder of the true nature of God in Isaiah 55:8–9:

FOR MY THOUGHTS are not your thoughts, Neither are your ways My ways declares the Lord. As far as the heavens are higher than the earth, So are My ways higher than your ways, And My thoughts than your thoughts.

IT DOESN'T MATTER what leads us to a consideration of God, whether His creation, His Word, or through our times of prayer, we will always come to the same conclusion: God is God, and there is none like Him.

After speaking of his meditation and his consideration of God, the Psalmist goes on to explain his relationship with God's statutes, or specific Laws. The Law doesn't naturally seem to me like something particularly special or desirable. In fact, the Law reminds me of my sin and limits my freedoms. For the Psalmist, however, the statutes of God were his delight. They weren't something he endured. They weren't something he simply put-up with. They weren't something he considered when it was convenient. No, the statutes brought delight to his heart. Delight is one of those *big* words; it means emotions such as glee, gladness, enchantment, satisfaction, relishing, or savoring. Is that how we approach God's Word? To be honest, when I read the precious promises of God, or when a certain passage affirms an area of growth that I've already achieved, I would tell you that the Word is absolutely, positively a delight. However, when the Word is convicting, or when an exhortation to

change is a hard pill to swallow, delight probably isn't the
first Word I'd choose to describe my reaction. For the
Psalmist, there was no hesitation: *His delight was in the
statutes of his God.*

The final action taken by the Psalmist is the action of
remembering God's Word. In fact, the language of this last
sentence of the passage indicates that the Psalmist is making
a verbal commitment that he will remember all that he has
heard from God. It's not: *I might, I hope to, maybe I will,* but
rather, he proclaims his commitment that he will remember
with the words: *I shall.* As we've discussed before, we are a
forgetful people. With this forgetfulness in mind, how can
we remind ourselves to remember God's Word? The answer
is a simple one; we must commit to hiding God's Word in
our hearts because we realize that it will protect us from sin.
Earlier in Psalm 119, the Psalmist states:

*THY WORD HAVE I treasured in my heart, that I might not sin
against Thee. –Psalm 119:11*

IF THERE IS one sure way to cloud our joy, it's by allowing
unconfessed sin to stand between us and God. Psalm 119:11
provides us with the remedy to that problem. When we treasure God's Word and hide it in our hearts, that Word
provides a protective mechanism to keep us from sinning.
The Holy Spirit uses that memorized Scripture to convict us
and to give us the opportunity to walk away from sin. Even
when no one is watching, God's Word, hidden in our hearts,
will remind us that God is always aware of our actions,
thoughts, and words.

The memorized Word of God truly is a treasure in so

many ways. It convicts us of sin, but it also encourages and comforts our hearts. God's Word can give us the direction we need when the path ahead is confusing. It can remind us of God's faithfulness to those whom He loves. It can answer our questions and calm our wandering thoughts. Obviously, reading the Word can accomplish all of those things, as well. However, when we don't have access to our Bibles, memorized Scripture is always on hand. Although technology has made it easier than ever to find verses on any topic, *"Hey Siri ... Show me all the verses on prayer."* the very discipline of memorizing Scripture will still produce great spiritual fruit and joy.

Quite frankly, my most productive memorization is the Scripture that I have memorized that directly addresses my own sin appetites. I'll just be honest with you, although I'm generally a pretty laid-back and unflappable personality, when I'm running behind or not completing my to-do list, I can have a very sharp tongue. I've said things in haste that have taken an inordinate amount of time to repair. Memorizing Scripture about my tongue has been such a valuable tool. When I'm tempted to speak unkindly, I don't need anyone else to say, "Slow down and think!" The Word of God that is hidden in my heart pricks my conscience and reminds me to speak words that are helpful, rather than hurtful.

Is memorizing Scripture a tedious task or a treasure in your life? When we understand the joy that God's Word hidden in our hearts can impart to our lives, we'll begin to recognize the true treasure that comes from the spiritual discipline of memorization. Grab your concordance, (or Google) find some verses to encourage and uplift your heart, or address your sinful appetites, and begin the adventure of filling your heart with the precious Word of God.

Psalm 19:7–9 continues the same theme concerning the fruit that is produced by carefully following the Word. Here, David explains the specific positive results that come from the different aspects of God's Word. Each of these varied facets of the Word combine to produce the fruit that is necessary to live joyful and productive Christian lives:

THE LAW of the Lord is perfect, restoring the soul;
  The testimony of the Lord is sure, making wise the simple.
  The precepts of the Lord are right, rejoicing the heart;
  The commandment of the Lord is pure, enlightening the eyes.
  The fear of the Lord is clean, enduring forever;
  The judgments of the Lord are true; they are righteous
altogether.

KING DAVID BEGINS his pronouncements by assuring his listeners that the Law of the Lord is perfect. That Law, although it oftentimes brings condemnation for sin, is the very thing that we need to restore our souls. Without the clarity of the Old Testament Law, men would not have recognized their own sinfulness. They would have recklessly done, as is recorded in Judges 17:6, *Whatever was right in their own eyes.* Recognizing our sin is the first step in realizing our need for a Savior. The Law is the road to restoring our souls.

I find it so interesting that it is the Law of God, not His promises, that restore the soul. As we pursue a deep understanding of God's Law, our way will be made sure, or stable. When are walking in a stable manner, God will give us wisdom and understanding, and that wisdom and understanding will bring joy to our hearts.

I absolutely hate the sensation of being unstable or insecure. When I turned fifty, suddenly the cheap cheater glasses from the drugstore weren't enough to help me see anymore. I found myself in prescription glasses with progressive lenses. For weeks, I felt as though I was on a roller coaster just walking across the kitchen floor. My depth perception was off, and I tripped both up and down the stairs. I misjudged doorways and smashed my shoulder into the side of the door more often than I could count. Trying to play tennis was a joke! I either swung over the ball or under the ball. I continually missed it altogether. During that transition to progressive lenses, I learned to rely heavily on solid markers. I looked intently at the lines on the road. I began to follow the pattern of our floors to recognize when I needed to step down. I carefully counted steps in order to keep from tumbling headlong. (Tennis? I just quit trying!)

Those markers acted as laws to govern my movements and keep me stable. They were boundaries that provided security and kept me from falling. As I learned to trust the limits they provided, my ability to function normally with those progressive lenses was restored. That's exactly how God's Law operates for us. His markers and boundaries restore our soul and keep us from falling. Wisdom and understanding work hand-in-hand with God's Law to show us our path.

As we previously observed in Psalm 19:7–9, God's testimony is what makes the simple wise. Honestly, we are the simple ones! God's testimony is what makes everything in this confusing world finally make sense. His testimony gives us the understanding we need to make wise and God-honoring decisions. When left to our own devices, we will behave like simpletons.

Next, David reassures his listeners that God's precepts

are right. Those precepts bring rejoicing to our hearts. Sometimes, we don't understand God's ways. His counter-intuitive instructions just don't seem to make any sense. However, based on His nature and character, we can rest peacefully in the knowledge that even when we don't under-stand, His precepts are always right.

Much like the Law of the Lord, His commandments bring light to our eyes. When our eyes are opened to the light, we will be able to discern between what is pure and what is impure. Although there are definitely areas of sin that I'm already aware of in my life, the Word of the Lord makes obvious those areas that *aren't* quite so noticeable. Parenting provides some clear examples of how this concept works in real life. Many times, I only realized the sinful bent of my children's hearts after I had set a parameter of obedi-ence before them. Without the call to obedience, they were perfectly happy, and I had no idea what was going on in their heart. But when the obedience I was requiring of them didn't suit their fancy ... Suddenly their true heart condition was very obvious to me.

Quite honestly, this same concept is evident in my own life. My husband is a Road Warrior. Or, since he's an airline pilot, I guess you could say he's an Air Warrior. Before becoming an airline pilot, he was in the Navy. For our entire married life, he's been away frequently. (Like ALL the time.) When he's gone, I'm basically the best wife around! I don't get impatient with him. I don't poo-poo his ideas. I don't get annoyed that he's following me from room to room. I don't hide in the bathroom to get some alone time. When he's gone, I can very easily live out Ephesians 5:22 and I Peter 3:1 ... *respecting a husband* who isn't home is a piece of cake for this girl! But then, Steve comes home. It's in those moments that God's commandments open my eyes to my own sinful attitudes. Without the Word of God to bring conviction to my heart, I'd continue patting myself on my *Aren't-I-The-Best-Wife-Ever* back! At the same time, however, I'd be prolonging my trek down the road of disrespect. God's Word brings the change that is so needed in my heart and our home.

When we think of what will endure forever, usually the first thing that comes to my mind is the souls of mankind. Whether in heaven with the Lord or cast into hell, men's souls are eternal by their very nature. In Psalm 19, however, David reminds us that the fear of the Lord endures forever. That type of reverential fear is exactly what we need to produce in us a desire to be cleansed from our sin. Too often, we allow unconfessed sin to simply be swept under the rug of our busyness. When sin is left to fester and infect, it affects every area of our lives. But, when we confess that sin and are freed from the weight of that sin, we can finally know what it feels like to be spiritually clean. Once we've truly experienced cleansing from sin and renewed intimacy with God, we'll fear ever again losing that sense of unsoiled relationship.

Finally, as we embrace the Law, testimony, precepts, commandments, and fear of the Lord, we will no longer dread or disregard His judgments. Instead, we will begin to welcome His true judgment of our thoughts, words, actions, and intentions. We will welcome His judgment because we will desire the righteousness that He provides. Truly, following God's Word obediently is the straight path for joyfully living this Christian life.

The second specific action of obedience which will produce Biblical joy goes hand-in-hand with following God's Word. Trusting God is what gives us the confidence that what He says is true. Trusting that He loves us and

desires good things for us will be a safeguard for our hearts
when the inevitable struggles come our way. Trusting His
good purposes for us will make His commandments a joy,
not a burden. Trusting God simply means believing Him;
taking Him at His Word, regardless if we understand all–or
any–that He wants to accomplish in our lives. Consider the
outcome of this type of trust and belief, as seen in Romans
15:13:

NOW MAY the God of hope fill you with all joy and peace in believing, that you may abound in hope by the power of the Holy
Spirit.

PAY close attention to the progression of events in this verse.
As we show our trust in God through believing, He grants us
joy and peace as a result of our belief. Then, our joy and
peace provide us with the opportunity to abound with hope.
Abounding is a beautiful word. We love to be with
abounding people. Abounding simply means to overflow.
There's nothing stingy or begrudging about abounding. It's
an open-handed, open-hearted pouring out of hope that is
made available to us through the work of the Holy Spirit.
That's the kind of Christian woman that I want to be! I want
my trust in God to produce abounding hope so that I can
pour out hope to those whom I love with an overflowing
and generous heart.

Let's look at one more action of obedience before we
close out this chapter. I know it's a lot to digest, but understanding clearly how and what to obey will help us to be
successful in our obedience. Success in our obedience

provides fertile soil for God to plant and reap more joy in our lives.

We can schedule time in the Word. We can certainly plan and schedule times of prayer. We can memorize God's Word whenever we have a few stolen moments of unfilled time. However, how do we schedule intimate times of simply resting in God's presence. For me, the *doing* actions of spiritual discipline are always easier to maintain than the *being* actions. Planning measurable acts of growth is a fairly straightforward process. But ... being in the presence of God? If I'm not carefully setting aside time to linger in God's presence, the lack of intimate relationship begins to affect every area of my life.

Psalm 16:8–11 has been an influential passage of Scripture for me as I strive to slow down and prioritize relational time with the Lord:

I HAVE SET the Lord continually before me; Because He is at my right hand, I will not be shaken. Therefore, my heart is glad, and my glory rejoices; My flesh also will dwell securely. For Thou wilt not abandon my soul to Sheol; Neither wilt Thou allow Thy Holy One to undergo decay. Thou wilt make known to me the path of life; In Thy presence is fulness of joy; In thy right hand there are pleasures forever.

Wow! Is that passage full of rich promises, or what? When I consider this Scripture, it becomes clear to me that being in God's presence isn't necessarily a scheduled activity, rather it is a purposeful awareness of God's continual attendance with my soul.

In context, this Psalm is quite clearly speaking of the resurrection of Jesus. In the book of Acts, both Paul and Peter referred to Psalm 16 and applied it to the life and death of Christ. However, as co-heirs with Christ, (Romans 8:17) we, also, have the precious promise of God presence. His presence is not only before us and beside us, it is within us in the person of the Holy Spirit. The third member of the Trinity ensures that our flesh can dwell securely and our confidence cannot be shaken. The result of such knowledge, according to the Psalmist, is a heart that is glad and a joy that rejoices.

As we abide in the presence of the Lord, we will discover the path of life. This certainly doesn't mean that we'll know exactly what's going to happen for the rest of our lives, but we will have confidence in our next step. This idea is echoed in Psalm 119:105 in reference to the Word of God being *a lamp for our feet*. Let me encourage you to discipline your mind and focus simply on the path of life that is next for you. So often, we worry and fret about what lies ahead. Elizabeth Elliot was well-known for exhorting believers to simply *Do the next thing*. May I add to that statement the reminder that worrying about the next-to-next thing never qualifies as the *next thing*.

Someday, we'll be with Jesus in heaven forever. That will be the ultimate fulness of joy for us. However, in the meantime as we inhabit these earthly bodies, our times of simply *being* in God's presence will give us a glimpse of that fulness. The words of the old hymn, *It Will Be Worth It All*, penned by Esther Kerr Rusthoi, often run through my head. The words strengthen my resolve to glorify Jesus in my daily life while filling my heart with longing to be with Him forever. Please allow me to share the beautiful words of the song with you.

· · ·

SOMETIMES THE DAY SEEMS LONG,
    Our trials hard to bear.
    We're tempted to complain,
    To murmur and despair.
    But Christ will soon appear
    To catch his bride away!
    All tears forever over
    In God's eternal day!

CHORUS:
    It will be worth it all
    When we see Jesus!
    Life's trials will seem so small
    When we see Christ.
    One glimpse of his dear face,
    All sorrow will erase.
    So, bravely run the race
    Till we see Christ.

AT TIMES the sky seems dark,
    With not a ray of light;
    We're tossed and driven on,
    No human help in sight.
    But there is One in heaven,
    Who knows our deepest care;
    Let Jesus solve your problems,
    Just go to him in prayer.

LIFE'S DAY will soon be o're,
    All storms forever past;

We'll cross the great divide
To Glory, safe at last!
We'll share the joys of heaven:
A harp, a home, a crown;
The tempter will be banished,
We'll lay our burdens down.

IT'S easy to casually say, "God's got it." but the flippant words don't do justice to the tremendous truth behind that statement. God does *Got It*! There is nothing He doesn't see and no trial that catches Him by surprise. We truly can relax in the safety and stability of our relationship with God.

Romans 8:19–23 reminds us that it's natural to *long to be present with the Lord*. In fact, *all of creation anxiously awaits* that day. Until then, let's be faithful in our obedience and rest with the Lord. When we learn to do that, we'll begin to reap the fulness of His joy and the pleasures He offers his children.

PERSONAL APPLICATION:

- In your reading of the Word this week, what specific calls to obedience have you discovered? Record them below.

- Have you ever found yourself in a situation in which your only call to obedience was the command to wait? In a few sentences, describe that waiting period and the spiritual fruit that it produced in your life.

- Where and when do you find yourself in God's presence. Do you seek His presence regularly? May I encourage you to pray (and write down if you'd like) a prayer of commitment to the action of seeking the Lord continually.

- Pick one of the verses that we've considered this week and commit it to memory. Keep reviewing your past verses ... You're doing great! ☺

7

MAKING OBEDIENCE YOURS

While other worldviews teach us to sit in the midst of life's joys,
foreseeing the coming sorrows, Christianity empowers its people
to sit in the midst of this world's sorrows, tasting the coming joy. –
Timothy Keller

I t's time to study a few more areas of the practical obedience that will increase our joy. Aren't you glad that the Word of God gives us some specific direction when it comes to obedience? I know my own heart, and if I were left to my own devices, I'd figure out which areas of obedience were the easiest and leave it at that. Thankfully, God's Word continues to challenge and grow me in this area. I hope it does the same for you!

In the last chapter, we discussed the importance of following the Word of God. However, it's nearly impossible to follow something we don't understand. As we take the time and invest the hard work that is necessary to truly understand what the Word is teaching us, we will be enabled to successful obey the truths it conveys. Obedience and joy go hand-in-hand, so understanding the Word is imperative.

As we already discovered through the teaching of the prophet Jeremiah, God's Word is not hidden from us. Not only can it be found, but as we internalize that Word, it will become the joy and delight of our hearts. Understanding God's Word takes more than a simple cursory reading. May I encourage you to fit time into your schedule to *study* the Word of God? Technology has made it so easy to do word searches and to look up the historical information that will help us to understand the context of a passage. Remember, the Scriptures were written to real, living people. There is a context that was applicable to the early church that isn't necessarily applicable today. However, if we skip over the original context and try to consider the Scripture based only on our 21st century understanding of the world, we will do a disservice to the Word, and we won't gain a clear understanding of what we read. Studying the Bible is definitely challenging, but it's an exciting challenge that brings about eternal benefits.

Part of understanding the Word is realizing that hearing, reading, and even studying the Bible will only be as effective as the application we bring to what we learn. Both in the Gospels and in the book of James, we are exhorted to be application-focused believers. In the book of Luke, Jesus said this to the crowd that was following Him:

BUT HE SAID, *"On the contrary, blessed are those who hear the word of God, and observe it."–Luke 11:28*

. . .

JAMES, another half-brother of Jesus, who after his salvation became the head of the church at Jerusalem, had this to say:

But PROVE yourselves doers of the word, and not merely hearers who delude themselves. For if anyone is a hearer of the word and not a doer, he is like a man who looks at his natural face in a mirror; for once he has looked at himself and gone away, he has immediately forgotten what kind of person he was. But one who looks intently at the perfect law, the law of liberty, and abides by it, not having become a forgetful hearer but an effectual doer, this man shall be blessed in what he does. –James 1:22–25

TRUE UNDERSTANDING of God's Word involves applicable action. Obedience and understanding are so closely linked in the life of the believer. When we choose to hear, but not to obey, we open the door wide for Satan to condemn and accuse us. (Revelation 12:10) At the same time, we make ourselves liable for the chastisement of the Lord. In truth, such discipline is a sure indication of how deeply He loves us, but as Hebrews 12:11 reminds us, *no discipline seems pleasant.*

Our biblical actions are often the best indicator of our understanding of the Word. Whether good or evil, our actions do not go unnoticed by our Heavenly Father. Thankfully, both the Lord Jesus and his half-brother James make the same unconditional promise to us: observe the Word, be a doer of the Word, and we shall be blessed.

Just for a moment, let's linger with a thought from the previous paragraph. Let me repeat it for clarity's sake: *As always, our actions do not go unnoticed by our Heavenly Father.* Many, many pages ago, I mentioned all of the responsibilities that we fill on a daily basis. We cook, we clean, we kiss boo-boos, we tuck children into bed, (And re-tuck them as often as it takes!) we prioritize our husbands, train our children, and minister to our friends. We basically pour ourselves out for others throughout our days. But sometimes, it seems like **No. One. Notices!** All of our acts of service for the benefit of others may go without acknowledgement or any expressions of gratitude. Still, for the most part, we just keep-on-keeping on because it's the right thing to do.

That paradigm couldn't be further from the truth when it comes to our loving God. There is no act of obedience that He misses! There is no sacrificing of self-will in order to honor Him that goes unnoticed. There is no repentant confession of sin to which He doesn't respond, no prayer He doesn't answer, and no true act of praise and worship that *He doesn't inhabit.* (Psalm 22:3) I believe with all my heart that God is aching to bless our obedience. That blessing comes in many ways, but perhaps one of the sweetest ways is through the promised joy that He brings to our hearts and lives. Dear sisters, *don't grow weary of doing well* when no one seems to notice. (Galatians 6:9) Instead, press on in the obedience of your faith, trusting that your gracious, Heavenly Father sees and is delighted by your *living and holy sacrifice.* (Romans 12:1)

Our acts of obedience are never for naught. As the Apostle Paul recorded, every Biblical change we make and every sinful appetite we conquer helps us *to press on toward the goal for the prize of the upward call of God in Christ Jesus.* (Philippians 3:14) Our eager obedience bears fruit in our own personal lives and in the lives of those around us. The beautiful end result of our good works and joyful obedience will be that *men will see our good works and glorify our Father who is in heaven.* (Matthew 5:16) That is why, regardless of the scope of our influence and the size of our circle of relationships, each and every one of us can impact the world for Christ.

Let me take another side road for a moment. You may have noticed that as I discuss obedience, I often use the word *eager.* For some of you who have read my other books, this explanation is going to be old news. However, I don't think there will be any harm done in reviewing the concept as I explain to new readers just what I mean by *eager.*

In the same way that there is a vast difference between joy and happiness, there is a difference between eager actions and willing actions. God wants us to be eager participants in our own spiritual growth! That means that we need to be eager in Bible reading, prayer, service, memorizing Scripture, and all of the other myriad growth-responsibilities of the Christian life. However, sometimes all that we offer to God is a willing spirit. We're willing to grow if the pastor makes a really good point. We're willing to pray if there's a really big need. We're willing to serve if no one else volunteers. Willing Christians can get things done, but often they miss the blessing obtained by eager obedience.

Eagerness is a proactive choice, not a reactive response. Let me explain. Imagine, for a moment, that I am in the 38th week of my seventh pregnancy. While walking into the house after a doctor's appointment, I trip over air (Literally ... over air! Insert eye roll) and break my ankle. Suddenly, I find myself an extremely pregnant woman, stuck on the couch with a bulky cast on my leg, and trying to corral my six young children. (Can you tell this is a true story?) Through the church prayer email, you find out about my predicament. You think to yourself, "That poor pathetic woman!" ('Cause I am!) Then, you pick up the telephone, reach out to me, and say, "I'm so sorry! If you need anything, give me a call and just let me know." If this scenario sounds like you, I would describe you as a willing friend. You're happy to assist if asked, but the onus is on me to initiate the request for help.

By contrast, an eager friend approaches the same lousy circumstance in a totally different manner. An eager friend is the one who calls and announces, "You poor thing! I'm headed over with a hot dinner and a second meal to put in your freezer. Can I pick up anything for you on the way? While you're waiting for me to arrive, think of some things I can do to help around the house. I'm planning on cleaning your toilets and sinks while I'm there, but would you like me to bathe the children, too?" That, my friends, is what eagerness looks like, and wouldn't we love to be surrounded by eager friends like that?!

Now, let's move willingness and eagerness into the spiritual realm. Although, to be honest, I'm pretty sure that the women who scrubbed my grimy toilets and bathed my stinky toddlers were actually participating in a *spiritual service of worship*! (Romans 12:1) Spiritual eagerness means that we don't wait to be coaxed and cajoled into obedience. We're attuned to the moving of the Holy Spirit in our hearts and we're always on the lookout for needful areas of growth and change. When we realize that an area of our life isn't pleasing to the Lord, we make prayerful and practical changes in order to put-off the old man and put-on the new man. We don't stay as close to the line of sin as possible, but instead, as I Timothy 6:11 instructs, we *Flee from these things, ... and pursue righteousness, godliness, faith, love, perseverance, and godliness.* When we sense that our spiritual joy is under attack, we act quickly in order to protect our joy immediately.

In a very real sense, becoming an eager participant in our own spiritual growth means becoming more like the prophet Samuel who, when he heard the Lord's voice, immediately responded, *Here, am I!* (I Samuel 3:4) He then followed that response with, *Speak, for Thy servant is listening.* (I Samuel 3:10) When we can become that type of eager servant of the Lord, attuned to His voice and prepared to obey, our lives will be changed and our joy will be full.

Sometimes, the scope of our acts of obedience is going to be focused on bringing good into the lives of other people. Consider what Proverbs 12:20 says:

DECEIT IS *in the heart of those who devise evil, But counselors of peace have joy.*

WHEN I FIRST READ THIS verse, my brain automatically wanted to switch the wording to *counselors of peace **bring** joy.* It seemed to make more sense that as we offer counsel with words of peace and comfort, those to whom we are counseling would walk away with joyful hearts. However, this is another one of those instances where we see how graciously God rewards us for our obedience. As we obediently bring the counsel of peace into someone else's life, God rewards us for our efforts by bringing joy into our own lives. It's the type of situation that is doubly sweet, as both the counselor and counselee walk away blessed by the Lord.

This type of obedience in the role of bringing peace to others entitles us to the precious title *son of God.* (Matthew 5:9) Coupled with an understanding of the Word, becoming a counselor of peace will afford the tremendous privilege of helping our Christian friends navigate difficult times. As well, prayerfully offered counsel may even provide us with the opportunity to point our unsaved friends to the Savior. Truthfully, being a peacemaker isn't always peaceful! There are times that we must, in obedience to the Lord and His Word, speak hard truths to one another. However, as we speak those truths *in love*, (Ephesians 4:15) the Holy Spirit can make our words acceptable and use them to minister help and hope.

If there is one area of obedience that seems to trip us up more than any other, I would guess that it is the area of surrender to God. When the Holy Spirit makes it clear that I need to put-off an area of life in order to honor God, generally speaking, I'm a fairly eager participant in that process. However, when it's an area of relationship with someone I love, or an area that is connected to what I refer to as a *Pet Sin*, the process is much more complicated. I find my will in a tug-of-war with God's will, even though I know that I will have no peace, no rest, and especially, no joy until I surrender!

Has God ever asked you to surrender something that you Just Really Loved? How did you respond? To be perfectly honest, I'm hopeful that at this stage in my life, there aren't *too* many things or activities that I wouldn't be ready to surrender. However, when it comes to giving up a relationship that I cherish but which doesn't glorify God, I still find it very difficult to raise the white flag of surrender.

It's been over twenty years now, but even writing about one of those surrender-the-relationship events still causes my stomach to churn. When I was a young mom, I developed a very close friendship with another woman in my church. She was a strong believer and a good mother, and we just really clicked from our very first meeting. Not only did we enjoy going places and doing things together with our children, we also had the type of friendship in which we could talk about deeply spiritual topics. Especially when Steve was gone for nine-month deployments with the Navy, this friendship was a lifeline for me.

Several years into our friendship, however, I began to sense that the Lord was troubling my heart about our relationship. I'm not a push-over, but I was definitely not the leader in our friendship. It was becoming obvious that when my friend shared strong opinions that weren't necessarily Biblical, I was choosing silence over discussion, debate, and possible disagreement. She wasn't particularly respectful of her own husband, and she certainly didn't encourage me to respect mine. In fact, as I shared–far too–intimate details about my marriage and some of the areas of change that my husband was encouraging me to make in my personal and spiritual life, she, too often, urged me to "Just tell him NO!" Besides the Holy Spirit bringing conviction to my heart, my husband let me know–in no uncertain terms–that this was an unhealthy friendship that really needed to end.

But I loved her. And I didn't want to hurt her. And I would miss our times together. And our kids loved each other. My list of excuses went on and on, and I sunk deeper and deeper into the murky waters of disobedience. It really wasn't until she made some very troubling changes in her doctrinal position and personal choices that I was finally able to end the relationship. By that point, the white flag of surrender was a sweet relief!

When we refuse to surrender, we place a roadblock in our relationship with God! We block His channel of blessing into our lives. It's as though we're stubborn preschoolers with our hands on our hips; defiantly declaring to the God of the universe, "You're not the boss of me!" I can say, from personal experience, the harder the area of surrender is to abandon, the greater the blessing when we submit to the Lord. Don't be afraid to surrender. Whatever God is asking us to give up is nothing compared to the wonderful blessings He wants to impart. Don't jeopardize your joy because of stubborn, stiff-necked pride that refuses to surrender! Consider this exhortation from Andrew Murray:

"WE HAVE HEARD IT BEFORE, but we need to hear it very definitely– the condition of God's blessing is absolute surrender of all into His hands. Praise God! If our hearts are willing for that, there is no end to what God will do for us, and to the blessing God will bestow."

WHAT A PRECIOUS REMINDER that our God is intent on blessing us. Our obedience opens the floodgates for that blessing! In light of that glorious truth, is there anything worth stubbornly clinging to and refusing to surrender to Him?

One more area, and then we can take a deep breath before we dive into the last two chapters about areas of obedience that produce joy. I know we've discovered a lot so far, but please don't be overwhelmed! These areas of obedience aren't like an action list that needs to be completed now, Now, NOW! Instead, they are actions that we will continue to *put-on* until we go to be with the Lord. They are continual, ongoing, (The geeky seminary word is *punctiliar*.) acts of growth and change that will carry on until we step from this life into glory. My life-verse is Philippians 1:6, and it provides great encouragement and comfort for our ongoing journey of submission, surrender, and obedience.

. . .

FOR I AM confident of this very thing, that He who began a good work in you will perfect it until the day of Christ Jesus.

IN OTHER WORDS, even on the days that I willfully fail to surrender, my faithful God will continue His work in my life. His good work will continue and be perfected in me when I go to be with Him. Not that I will attain perfection by any merit of my own, but I will attain it because of the gracious, patient, continual work of my God.

The final obedience that we'll consider is based solely on the character of God, but it is ineffectual in our lives without our participatory actions of recognition and obedience. One of the attributes of God is His trustworthiness. Because He is trustworthy, we can trust His Word, His actions toward us, and His promises. That trustworthiness demands our obedient response of hope in our God. Josh McDowell says this about the trustworthiness of God.

"WHEN CHRIST DECLARES, 'Trust me, I've got everything under control,' He doesn't say that in a vacuum. He says that amidst the storms of interruptions, irritations, ill treatment, disease, disaster and death, against the backdrop of His faithfulness and trustworthiness ... He doesn't forget about you and me."

THERE REALLY IS no hierarchy of priority when it comes to our obedience *to* God and our trust *in* God. Both actions are of the utmost importance in the mind of the Lord. Author Jerry Bridges puts it this way:

. . .

"YET, *it is just as important to trust God as it is to obey Him. When we disobey God, we defy His authority and despise His holiness. But when we fail to trust God we doubt His sovereignty and question His goodness. In both cases we cast aspersions upon His majesty and His character. God views our distrust of Him as seriously as He views our disobedience ... In order to trust God, we must always view our adverse circumstances through the eyes of faith, not of sense. And just as the faith of salvation comes through hearing the message of the gospel, so the faith to trust God in adversity comes through the Word of God alone. It is only in the Scriptures that we find an adequate view of God's relationship to and involvement in our painful circumstances. It is only from the Scriptures, applied to our hearts by the Holy Spirit, that we receive the grace to trust God in adversity."*

IN OTHER WORDS, if we want to please God, we must trust God. If we want to trust God, we will find the knowledge of His trustworthiness in His Word. Finally, putting that knowledge of trustworthiness into action will provide us with the strength we need to hope in God alone in our times or trial and adversity.

This concept of the joy experienced by the trustworthiness of our hope in God is found in Romans 12:9–14:

LET LOVE BE WITHOUT HYPOCRISY. *Abhor what is evil; cling to what is good. Be devoted to one another in brotherly love; give preference to one another in honor; not lagging behind in diligence, fervent in spirit, serving the Lord; rejoicing in hope, persevering in tribulation, devoted to prayer, contributing to the needs of the saints, practicing hospitality. Bless those who curse you; bless and curse not.*

. . .

IF WE WERE TRYING to find a list of actions that we should undertake as Christians, this section of the book of Romans would be a great starting point. As we consider these exhortations, however, it becomes obvious that some are seemingly easy to perform while others are just simply more difficult. Most of the time, it's not that hard to be devoted to those whom I love in a brotherly–or for us, sisterly–way. Contributing to the needs of others and practicing hospitality are as much a blessing for me as they are a service to others. Some things on the list just seem to make sense and they don't actually seem to be very personally costly.

However, some of these other action items are just plain hard! It's hard to persevere in tribulation. It's difficult to remain devoted to prayer when I don't see the answers to my prayers in what I consider to be a timely manner. Sometimes, it's downright impossible to force myself to bless those who persecute me. *Who Do They Think They Are, Anyway!!!*

However, tucked right in the middle of that list in Romans 8 is the key to living out the Lord's directives, whether easy or difficult. Verse 12 begins with this instructional command: *Rejoicing in hope.* Rejoicing in hope gives us the inward strength that is required to live this Christian life. Whether cheerfully practicing hospitality or bearing up under the weight of unjust persecution, the joy that is found through our hope in God will give us the spiritual fortitude that we need to press on, regardless of our circumstances.

The dictionary defines the word hope like this:

A FEELING *of expectation and desire for a certain thing to happen.*

. . .

WHEN WE HAVE expectations of people or circumstances, we will often find ourselves disappointed. But our expectant hope of the Lord and of His commitment to His promises will never disappoint us. We can place our hope on the finished work of Christ on our behalf. We can rest our hope in His promised good intentions toward us. And, we can anchor our hope on the expectation of our future home with Him in heaven. What a tremendous blessing we receive when we practice obedience in the area of hoping in our God!

PERSONAL APPLICATION:

- What practical tools are you utilizing in order to gain a deeper understanding of God's Word? Is there any area of your life in which it is clear that although you understand the Scriptures, you are failing to obey the Scriptures? If so, list practical steps that you can take to move from understanding to obedience.

- Being a peacemaker is difficult work. In a few sentences, describe a time that God used you to bring peace to a troubling situation. Were you able to infuse that interaction with joy?

- Surrendering something that is precious to us is so difficult! Can you recall a time that the Lord asked you to surrender something that was costly to you? In a few sentences, record what was required and how you responded to the Lord's direction.

- We can trust in God because He is always trustworthy! Is there any situation that seems hopeless right now? Spend a few moments jotting down a prayer to God. Ask for the strength to hope in Him as you trust Him to work in your seemingly hopeless situation.

- Don't forget to choose a memory verse to add to your list!

8

OBEDIENCE IS THE VERY BEST WAY TO SHOW THAT YOU BELIEVE

"He offers an exchange: His life for ours. He showed us what He meant by giving Himself. The overwhelming fact of the Son's obedience to the Father—hell itself harrowed by the Infinite Majesty—does it not call us far out of ourselves, far beyond the pitiful, calculating, cowardly, self-serving, self-saving pursuit of what the world calls happiness? He offers us love, acceptance, forgiveness, a weight of glory, fullness of joy. Is it so hard to offer back the gifts that came in the first place from the wounded hands—body, mind, place, time, possessions, work, feelings? –
Elizabeth Elliot

Okay, let's all take a deep breath before we take the plunge into these final two chapters about the obedient actions that will produce joy in our hearts. Trust me, once we've studied and understood the importance of obedience, the later chapters that discuss God's promises that produce joy will seem like icing on the cake. But before we get to God's part of the responsibility, it's imperative that we understand our part.

The ownership of our joy requires that we protect that joy by becoming wise. Following the Word and understanding the Word are only made complete as we acquire the wisdom found within the Word. Wisdom is God's Word made applicable to our lives. Such a wisdom will protect us from any onslaught that would threaten our joy, whether it be personal sin or trials brought on by others.

The Proverbs provide some clear direction in our search for joy-abounding wisdom. The Proverbs are considered *Didactic Wisdom Literature*. That's a $10.00 title that simple means that the Proverbs teach truths concerning what should happen in the normal turn of events. Proverbs 15:21 teaches an important distinction between the joy of believers and the joy of the unsaved:

FOLLY IS *joy to him who lacks sense, But a man of understanding walks straight.*

FOR THE PAST SIX CHAPTERS, we've been discovering that Christians must own their joy. At the same time, we have the personal responsibility to nurture and protect that joy. We've seen that joy is found in the person of Jesus Christ, and it begins with our salvation and will continue throughout eternity.

Not so the joy of the unsaved. According to Proverbs 15, the joy of the lost man is found in his folly. According to the dictionary, folly means *lack of good sense; foolishness.* The entire book of Proverbs paints a dark picture of the fool.

Such a man (or woman) makes choices willfully and sinfully. Fools aren't content to act alone, however, instead they draw others into their net of foolishness. They lack the sense to know that their end is death. (Proverbs14:12)

Considering the ultimate result end of the unsaved should cause our hearts to cry out, "Don't you see where you're headed!" But for the fool, Proverbs 15 makes it clear, the very actions that are leading them to eternal death are the actions that bring them joy. The wise man, on the other hand, seeks to know God and His ways. Psalm 16:11 clearly demonstrates the disparity of the foolishly joyful end of the unsaved and the wisdom-focused life of the believer.

THOU WILT MAKE KNOWN to me the path of life; In Thy presence is fulness of joy; In Thy right hand there are pleasures forever.

SEEKING wisdom and taking necessary steps of obedience is the pathway to fullness of joy. Time in the Word, prayer, and placing ourselves under sound Biblical teachers will help us to become wise Christians. However, wisdom isn't only found through our own personal spiritual disciplines. Wisdom is also found in the friendships that we choose and in the intimate relationships which we develop.

Proverbs 13:20 provides this promise and warning:

HE WHO WALKS with wise men will be wise, But the companion of fools will suffer harm.

. . .

FOR GOOD OR FOR EVIL, all of our relationships influence us. Either they will influence us to walk in obedience and grow in wisdom, or they will influence us to wander down the path of folly and sin. As we choose to *not forsake the assembling together*, (Hebrews 10:25) with Christ-honoring and Biblically-focused sisters-in-Christ, we will be encouraged and spurred on in our own growth in wisdom. Please allow me to ask you a question for contemplation. Are you developing friendships that exhort you toward growth in wisdom, or are you simply spending *fun* time involved in friendships that draw your heart away from Christ? True friendships take work, but that work should always build accountability and encourage mutual growth.

I think that this next area of obedience is one that most of us would already acknowledge as a necessary aspect of the Christian life. This area of obedience is our worship. However, I don't believe that we truly understand worship's relationship to joy. Worship is an act of obedience, but as such, it must be founded in and it must produce Biblical joy.

The Psalms are perhaps our most instructive section of Scripture when it comes to understanding the obedience of joyful worship. Whether penned by King David or the choir master, the Psalms present clearly the interrelationship between worship and joy, both the joy we find through worship and the reasons behind that joy. Consider Psalm 100:

SHOUT JOYFULLY TO THE LORD, *all the earth.*
  Serve the Lord with gladness;
  Come before Him with joyful singing.
  Know that the Lord Himself is God'
  It is He who has made us, and not we ourselves;

We are His people and the sheep of His pasture.

ENTER HIS GATES WITH THANKSGIVING,
    And His courts with praise.
    Give thanks to Him; bless His name.
    For the Lord is good;
    His lovingkindness is everlasting,
    And His faithfulness to all generations.

THERE IS SO much instruction for us packed into this one little Psalm. First of all, the Psalmist instructs God's people carefully so that we know just how we are to come before the Lord. We are to come with joyful shouts and songs. I get the impression that the Psalmist is reminding the people that their faces need to show on the outside the joy that they claim on the inside.

Psalm 100 explains the source of that joyful shouting and singing. It is based solely in the knowledge that the Lord Himself is God. That's enough! We don't need to focus on what He's done, how He's provided, what His plans for us are ... We just need to know that He is God. The Psalmist reminds the people of God's ownership of them *He made us* and his compassionate care for them *We are the sheep of His pasture*. These two truths only add to the joyful recognition of who God is and His relationship with us.

The second half of the Psalm switches from joy to thanksgiving. Thanksgiving is the natural overflow of a joyful heart. Again, the Psalmist reminds the listeners of the cause for that joy: God's goodness, His everlasting lovingkindness, and His faithfulness. What a wonderful

God we serve! Our joyful worship sounds aloud His goodness and character to all who hear.

When we forget that our worship belongs to God and is a matter of obedience, we will quickly begin to slide into a place of *ownership* of our worship. Any attempt to claim worship as something that we produce or present to God on our own is just another form of self-focused disobedience. Yikes! That's something we need to chew on ... If joyful worship is a matter of obedience, self-generated worship becomes an issue of sin. To walk faithfully with our God, our only choice is obedient and joyful worship *for* Him and *because* of Him.

Another area of obedience in which it becomes easy for us to take all the credit is the obedience of serving others. In our attempts to be the hands and feet of Jesus for others, it's so tempting to begin to commend ourselves for a job well done. When people compliment us for our sacrifice, or call us life-savers, or place us high on a pedestal of praise and flattery ... beware! Serving others is a precious gift from the Lord. Truthfully, He doesn't need us. If the God of the universe desired, He could minister to hurting people through a rock. Thankfully, He allows us the precious privilege of being His servants. I believe He grants us the privilege of service as an avenue to receive His joy and to express our gratitude for all that He has done for us.

It's so easy to limit our acts of service to doing those things that make us comfortable. Although there is certainly a blessing in performing acts of service that are within our comfort zone, the greatest joy is found when we abandon ourselves to whatever service the Lord has for us to undertake. Although my natural gifts are probably in the teaching and counseling realms, God has truly blessed me with His joy as I've scrubbed toilets, pulled weeds–unsuccessfully, at times–and hosted church parties and ladies fellowships (An introvert's nightmare...).

Consider what Philippians 2:1–7 teaches us about the command to serve one another.

IF THEREFORE THERE is any encouragement in Christ, if there is any consolation of love, if there is any fellowship of the Spirit, if any affection and compassion, make my joy complete by being of the same mind, maintaining the same love, united in spirit, intent on one purpose. Do nothing from selfishness or empty conceit, but with humility of mind let each of you regard one another as more important than himself; do not merely look out for your own personal interests, but also for the interests of others. Have this attitude in yourselves which was also in Christ Jesus, who although He existed in the form of God, did not regard equality with God a thing to be grasped, but emptied Himself, taking the form of a bond-servant, and being made in the likeness of men.

THE QUESTION with which Paul begins this passage of Scripture is rhetorical. The unequivocal answer to his question is *YES!* Because the life of the believer does consist of love, and fellowship, and affection, and compassion, we have all that we need to love and serve one another unselfishly. As we empty ourselves, we will then be filled by Christ Jesus. Our service will truly become an act of His service to others.

Sometimes, we're called to perform some act of service that simply doesn't interest us. Or, it seems somehow *below* us. Again, Christ is our example. As Philippians 2 teaches us, Christ didn't consider anything too lowly for Him to do. In fact, Jesus took the form of a bond-servant and became like us! I can hardly imagine the sacrifice involved in giving-up His existence in the form of God in order to be one of us.

After what the Lord has done for us is there anything too hard or lowly that we wouldn't do for Him? I appreciate how Elizabeth Elliot describes our obedience of service. Consider this quote from her book, *Discipline: The Glad Surrender*:

THERE IS no such thing as Christian work. That is, there is no work in the world which is, in and of itself, Christian. Christina work is any kind of work, from cleaning a sewer to preaching a sermon, that is done by a Christian and offered to God. This means that nobody is excluded from serving God. It means that no work is beneath a Christian. It means there is no job in the world that needs to be boring or useless. A Christian finds fulfill-ment not in the particular kind of work he does, but in the way in which he does it. Work done for Christ all the time must be 'full-time Christian work.'

WHAT THIS QUOTE tells me is that although I am involved in full-time Christian service through our Characterhealth ministry, I must also be fully attuned to and always available for my Master. When God shows me an area of service, I do not have the freedom to excuse myself from serving by reminding Him of Just. How. Much. I already do. Regardless of how impressed I am with myself, I'm fairly confident that God isn't impressed with my resume or rationalizations.

On the other hand, serving must be God-prompted and Spirit-enabled in order to produce Biblical results. If we want to experience the joy that comes from serving, our service must bring glory to God. That means that we won't wear ourselves out, running here and there, trying to be the answer to everyone's problems and needs-of-the-moment. Becoming a joy-producing servant of God requires us to be totally attentive to the leading of the Holy Spirit. Just because we *can* do something doesn't always mean we *should* do something. Prayerfully seeking the Lord's direction for our service will keep us from over-extending ourselves. It will also keep us from robbing others of the joy that God wants them to experience through service.

One final thought on service. Service is one of the greatest antidotes that we have to help us combat feelings of self-pity. Self-pity clouds joy. The problem with self-pity and throwing ourselves a pity party is the fact that no one else will join us. In fact, most people are so busy feeling sorry for themselves that they won't even notice how rough life is for us.

When trials are looming and circumstances are threatening your joy, may I encourage you to ask the Lord to provide you with an avenue of service. Even in my hardest trials, (And there have been some doozies!) God has faithfully shown me others who are going through even more difficult times of trial and testing. Finding practical ways to extend God's love to them through Christian service has been a blessing to them and medicine to my own heart.

Obedient service is a precious gift from God that is enveloped in the wrapping paper of joy. As we prayerfully and faithfully serve others, both in the family of God and those who don't yet know Jesus, we will be blessed and encouraged. Serving others will increase our joy while at the same time providing us with an opportunity to minister to others from a heart full of gratitude to our Lord.

Serving out of obedience to the Lord isn't onerous. Instead, serving the One who sacrificed so much to provide for our salvation becomes an offering of gratitude and thanksgiving. How wretched indeed would we find ourselves without the outlet of service to show our Lord just how much He means to us and how thankful we are for His love toward us.

PERSONAL APPLICATION:

- Considering the necessity of acquiring wisdom, what steps are you taking to make your head knowledge applicable in your daily life? Record those steps below. Recording what you are doing will give you a clear indication of whether or not your head knowledge has truly become heart and action knowledge.

- How do you worship the Lord? Worship is about so much more than just singing. Record below some of your favorite helps for worship. Is there anything that you feel is lacking in your worship? If so, spend some time praying and asking the Lord to show you how to obediently and joyfully worship Him.

- In the space provided, jot down both the areas of service in which you are currently involved and any areas of service which are outside your comfort zone but which you believe God would have you undertake. After recording both categories, seek the Lord in prayer, asking His wisdom as you take on new actions of service.

- It's time to choose another memory verse. You're building quite a storehouse of God's Word in your heart!

IF WE LOVE GOD WE'LL OBEY GOD

*A*nd every one of us is a temple of God, in which God will dwell and work mightily on one condition—absolute surrender to Him. God claims it. God is worthy of it, and without it God cannot work His mighty work in us.

—Andrew Murray

WE MADE IT! This is the final chapter of the *obediences* that will open the floodgates for God to pour out His blessing of joy on us. Now is as good a time as any to give us all a quick reminder. Consider this an important safety tip from Mama Megan to you ... *Learning to walk in obedience isn't a sprint; it's a marathon.*

If you're anything like me, each year on January 1st, you set yourself some New Year's Resolutions. (Except I like to call them *God-Focused Goals* 'cause I'm all spiritual like that ... you can insert your own eye roll on that one.) And, every year like clockwork, by the middle of February, those goals are old news and I'm basically back to my normal and sluggardly ways.

Was it that my goals were bad? Is it unreasonable to expect myself to change? Nope! However, when I try to change too many areas at once, I'm simply setting myself up for failure. The same concept holds true as we approach our spiritual life and begin to walk in obedience in these areas that we had perhaps never considered before.

My sweet friends, God is not like an Olympic High Jump coach who is continually raising the bar! Instead, He is *compassionate and gracious, slow to anger and abounding in lovingkindness.* (Psalm 103:8) He doesn't poke or prod us. He doesn't say, "That was good, but now I expect more." Rather, He blesses our smallest steps of obedience and encourages us on our way. The Christian life of obedience is as Eugene Peterson said, *A long obedience in the same direction.*

One of the things that really struck me when I had the opportunity to travel to Israel was the tremendous number of heaped up rocks that we encountered. As we traveled throughout the countryside, everywhere there were more heaps. Those piled up rocks represented something to the ancient Jew. The rocks were purposefully placed there as a memorial. Whether it was to remember God's faithfulness toward them or to memorialize a commitment that they had made to their God, the ancient Jews realized the importance of building a memorial of remembrance. When we see victory in an area of obedience, I think it is just as important for us to find a way to memorialize, or remember, those moments of victory. In our rush to move on to the next *to-do* of obedience, we weary ourselves by not stopping to celebrate growth and change.

Now obviously, piling up rocks around your house isn't going to make sense in this current culture, (Although I do think your neighbors might ask some great questions about your rocks ...) but still it's important to find ways to recognize and celebrate growth. As we, in a sense, build those memorials, they will become a tangible reminder in times when we need some reassurance that we truly are growing and changing. When joy is difficult to see because of our trials, our memorials will rejuvenate our joy-starved hearts. I mentioned before that I underline and date specific commands of obedience in my Bible. For me, those dated and underlined passages provide the memorial reminders that I need to keep on keeping on! How will you build memorials to growth?

As we consider the acts of obedience from the last three chapters, as well as the four new ones we will discover in this chapter, our first response should be to seek the Lord in prayer. We can trust Him to show us which acts are needful for us in this moment. As we faithfully obey the leading of the Holy Spirit and begin to experience victory in those areas of obedience, we will be preparing ourselves for obedience in areas that are, for us, more difficult. Only then will our growth be, as recorded in Isaiah 28:10, *Order on order, line on line, a little here and a little there.* Instead of being characterized by stop and go, high and low, starts and restarts, our spiritual life will become a slow, steady upward walk of faithful change and growth. Let's finish strong with four more acts of obedience that will glorify our God and bring joy in our Christian journey.

This next area of obedience is a hard one to quantify. We can track our acts of service and we can record our growth in understanding and following the Word.

And you'd better believe, I have a serious mental record of the times I've been called to surrender something that I love. But just as important as those measurable areas of obedience are, of equal importance and often overlooked, is our obedience to faithfully abiding in Christ.

The word *abide* is defined this way:

To REMAIN *stable and fixed in a state; to continue in a place*

PERHAPS THE BEST synonym for abide is the word *sojourn*. Abiding with Christ means that we are stable in our relationship with Him. We are fixed in a state of trust and dependency. There is great peace in abiding. Quite frankly, this area of obedience is a difficult one for me. Although I may outwardly appear to be quietly sojourning with Jesus, too often my anxious thoughts are pacing the room while I'm inwardly wringing my hands.

This concept of abiding is clearly seen in Psalm 46:10, when the Psalmist says:

CEASE STRIVING *and know that I am God.*

THE ONLY WAY that we can truly calm our anxious thoughts and quiet our restless souls is by knowing, in the absolute truest sense of the word, that God is God. He made us, He loves us, He cares for us, and He will provide for us and protect us. When I am abiding with Christ, I am in the safest shelter possible!

Jesus Himself recognized the need for the disciples to realize the importance of abiding with Him. During His last pre-resurrection meal with the twelve, while he was reclining at the table, Christ shared some final essential truths with these men who had accompanied Him for so long. In the midst of exhorting them to love one another and reminding them that He would return for them, our Lord took the time to stress the importance of abiding with both God the Father and Jesus Himself. In John 15: 9–11, Jesus taught this important principle about the co-relationship between obedient abiding and the resultant joy:

JUST AS THE *Father has loved Me, I have also loved you; abide in My love. If you keep My commandments, you will abide in my love; as I have kept My Father's commandments, and abide in His love. These things I have spoken to you, that My joy may be in you, and that your joy may be made full.*

NOTICE THAT IN THIS PASSAGE, the disciples are not being called to abide in the Lord's commandments. Instead, their obedience in following the commandments is what opens the door for abiding in His love. As the disciples obeyed and sojourned in the love of the Lord, their joy would be made full. Like the disciples in the upper room, the Lord's command for us to abide in Him is all about stable trust and dependency upon His love for us, and the resultant gift is His joy, freely bestowed on us.

Although we can't necessarily quantify and measure how well we are doing in the area of abiding, if abiding is missing in our relationship with the Lord, that lack will inevitably become obvious to everyone. Our inward anxiety will quickly become outward fretting. Our worried thoughts will become fearful preoccupations with the worst-case scenarios of life. Trust will be replaced by fear, and joy will be hidden by apprehension and uneasiness.

Abiding is essential if we desire to live joy-filled and Christ-trusting lives. Now would be a good time to do a little spiritual inventory of your thought life. Are your moments of quiet consumed with racing thoughts of impending trouble? If so, run to the Lord in prayer. Confess those anxious thoughts to Him and spend time in the Word, allowing His truth to comfort and strengthen you.

Interestingly, as we grow in our obedience of abiding, generosity will become the natural overflow of a transformed life. Regardless of our circumstances of the moment, becoming obedient in the area of generosity is necessary for us to experience the full joy of our inheritance in Christ. As we learned previously, the book of Philippians is a book about abounding joy. The circumstances in which the Philippian believers found themselves weren't conducive to joy, but their deep love relationship with the Lord produced overflowing joy in spite of those very hard circumstances.

While writing to the Corinthian believers, the Apostle Paul referred to these joyful and generous Philippian believers, as well as the believers in Thessalonica and Berea, when he praised the Macedonian churches saying:

Now, brethren, we wish to make known to you the grace of God which has been given in the churches of Macedonia, that in a great ordeal of affliction their abundance of joy and their deep poverty overflowed in the wealth of their liberality. – II Corinthians 8:1–2

. . .

IN THIS PASSAGE, Paul links what seems to be two contrary and opposite concepts. In writing about the offering that was gathered by the Macedonian believers, Paul sets the stage by reminding the Corinthians that these believers were undergoing great affliction. However, the disparate combination of their joy and poverty in that ordeal of afflic- tion resulted in an overflowing generosity toward fellow- sufferers. The Macedonian believers didn't check their bank accounts or 401Ks before they gave an offering. Instead, they dug deeply into their own meager purses and gave with praiseworthy liberality.

Such generosity is only possible when we trust in God to provide for our needs! I'm thankful that I'm married to a generous man. From the earliest days of our marriage, Steve has been a constant example of generosity. In fact, even when I worried about how we would make ends meet, Steve still led our family to give to those whom were less fortunate than we were. And do you know what happened? God ALWAYS provided for all of our needs! In fact, He has provided more than we could have ever hoped or imagined.

Steve's faithful generosity has paid huge dividends in the lives of all eight of our children. I can't even express the joy I experience as I watch them share generously with one another, their friends, and more often than not, strangers who they discover are in need. They have seen God provide for us, so they have no doubt that He will provide for them. I can't over-emphasize the importance of modeling generosity for your children! When their faith in God's provision is rock-solid, obeying God through generosity will be natural.

We can never *out-give* God. As we are generous toward others, God generously bestows His blessing of joy upon us. Let me add one small warning about this area of obedience, though. We can perform the physical act of giving to others, but we may miss out on the blessing of obedient generosity. Let me explain ...

Acts 5:1–11 is the recounting of the actions of a couple named Ananias and Sapphira. These two were believers and part of the early Christian church. As the Scripture teaches, the early church was known for how they cared for one another. When anyone was in need, that need would be met by a fellow believer. Into this context come Ananias and Sapphira. Although it would be easy to believe that the reason they were struck dead was that they didn't give all that they had to give ... such an understanding of the passage would be misleading. The leaders of the early church never demanded that the believers give everything that they owned; *giving was voluntary, not under compulsion.*

The problem with Ananias and Sapphira was the condition of their hearts. They wanted to give the impression of sacrificial giving. They wanted the other believers to think better of them than they deserved. As Peter reminds them in the passage, *the land they sold to get the money for their offering was theirs.* They had the right to decide how much they would give. The problem was their desire to be known for giving more than they actually gave. Generous, God-prompted giving turns the spotlight on God; it never draws attention to itself.

Obedient and generous giving isn't about how much we give. Those who have little to give are sometimes the most generous Christians. Instead, it's always about the attitude of the heart. When God says *Give,* our only response should be *"How much Lord?"* We can trust Him to provide for our needs. When we have that type of trust in God, we truly will be able to become joyful givers.

There is joy in obediently serving the Lord. However, in

Matthew 25:20–30, that concept of serving is narrowed to the application of work that is done faithfully for the Lord. Consider what this passage has to teach about the joy that is found in faithful work.

AND THE ONE who had received the five talents came up and brought five more talents, saying, 'Master, you entrusted five talents to me; see, I have gained five more talents.' His master said to him, 'Well done, good and faithful slave; you were faithful with a few things, I will put you in charge of many things, enter into the joy of your master.' The one also who had received the two talents came up and said, 'Master, you entrusted to me two talents; see, I have gained two more talents.' His master said to him, 'Well done, good and faithful slave; you

were faithful with a few things, I will put you in charge of many things; enter into the joy of your master.'

I'VE OFTEN CONSIDERED that repeated phrase from this section of Matthew: *Enter into the joy of your master.* What exactly does it mean to enter into the Lord's joy? Honestly, I think it goes back to the Jim Berg quote in Chapter One, *The kind of relationship God has in mind for us will mean that both the Creator and the creature find their greatest joy in the joy of the other."* I believe that as our obedient and faithful work for the Lord brings joy to His heart, we, too, shall share in that joy.

But what's the difference between *working* for the Lord and *serving* the Lord? For me, serving the Lord means that there is no task, large or small, that I'm not eager to perform at the prompting of the Lord. Service isn't really about what

I'm good at. Instead, it's about how available I am to be used by God. Not to be corny, but it's putting the little saying, *God wants my availability, not my ability* into action.

Faithful work for the Lord, on the other hand, involves devotedly working for the Lord by using the gifts and talents that He's given me. There are many, many *good* things that I enjoy doing as an offering to the Lord, but the *best* things that I can offer Him are the works done through faithful stewardship of my gifts. To be honest, some of those good things are more fun than the best things. There are good actions that I really enjoy doing. It isn't that I don't ever have the freedom to perform those good deeds, it's simply that faithful work for the Lord requires me to purposefully prioritize and utilize my gifts as directed by Him.

Let me try to explain what I mean in real life ... I LOVE feeding teens and children. If there's something that floats my boat, it's making menus, directing others, and leading a team to prepare tummy-warming food for kids. In other words, I love being a camp cook. I'm absolutely convinced that there is a direct correlation between the comforting security of a warm meal and well-filled tummy and the ability of children to hear the truth of the gospel. For ten years, I spent much of every summer working for the Lord in a Child Evangelism Fellowship camp kitchen. That was good work and I loved it.

However, as much as I love feeding kids, my real areas of giftedness are in the avenues of teaching, speaking, and communicating through writing and counseling. To be honest, sometimes those areas of giftedness just aren't very FUN. Sitting at a computer working on manuscripts is tiring and my eyes hurt! Preparing for conferences and packing up to travel is tiring and my back hurts! Counseling with hurting couples and grieving parents is tiring and my heart hurts! Do you get the picture? Sometimes using my gifts just hurts!

I don't really have a choice in the matter. If I want to experience the joy that comes from faithfully *using the talents* that the Lord has given to me, (Matthew 25) I must obediently do those things that exercise those talents. For ten years, I was able to obediently work for the Lord within my gifts while still finding time to lead the camp kitchen for several weeks each summer. That seemed like a pretty sweet deal to me. However, about five years ago, the Lord began to expand the scope of my work for Him. All of the sudden, I was forced to make a choice; would I say no to opportunities to work within my gifts just so that I could continue to happily cook at camp?

As hard as it is to give up something that seems good–something that in and of itself isn't inherently wrong–there are times in life that good and best just simply can't coexist. Although there were many other women who could run the camp kitchen just as efficiently as I could–probably better in some instances–there was no one else who could fill my shoes in the writing, speaking, and counseling ministry that God had called me to fulfill.

It isn't only *work* that provides an entrance into the joy of the Master. Rather, it is a commitment and involvement to the work that the Lord has particularly called us to perform. When we are faithful in that work, we will find great joy from the Lord. Remember when I mentioned that sometimes doing the work that God has gifted me to do can cause pain? What I failed to mention is that EVERY time that I'm faithful to fulfill that *best* work, there is blessing. When I am focused on faithfully working and glorifying God through that work, those to whom I minister are blessed, and I can personally sense the good pleasure of God.

But how can we know what work it is to which the Lord is calling us? Elizabeth Elliot provides a helpful perspective:

WHAT IS OUR 'PROPER SPHERE'? We cannot dismiss the fact of modern life: there are indeed many choices when it comes to discerning that sphere. Let us rest assured that God knows how to show His will to one who is willing to do it. The place to begin discovering the larger sphere is in the smaller one—in the willingness to say yes to every demand that the need of a neighbor makes us face.

IN OTHER WORDS, some of us are gifted for *Big Work*. God may place us before large audiences or provide us with a sizeable following. Others are gifted to perform more intimate works for the Lord. It isn't the size of our work that matters. What matters is a heart of obedience that is eager to work in order to faithfully utilize our gifts and talents. Every work, faithfully fulfilled out of obedience to God, will build our character, increase our joy, and move us along in our journey of growth and change.

It's here! We've reached the last action of obedience on our journey toward protecting and nurturing our God-given and Christ-focused joy. Of all the actions we've discussed thus far, this one is nearest and dearest to my heart. As I shared previously, when I came to know the Lord as my personal Savior, I truly experienced joy for the first time in my life. Accompanying that joy was a deep sense of thankfulness. I completely understood that I was a sinner. I was actually a fairly proficient sinner—quite good at my chosen sinfulness. I was thankful for my salvation. I was thankful that God could change me. I was thankful for new brothers and sisters in Christ. The list of *thankfulnesses* went on and on ...

To be honest, I've never lost that sense of thankfulness. Even in the midst of trials, and even when life seems like a deep gray bucket of yuck, that thankfulness has been a protection for my heart. Imagine my delight when in my study for this book, I discovered that thankfulness is one of avenues that God uses as He fills His people's hearts with joy.

Psalm 126 portrays the union of thankfulness and joy that was experienced by the people of Zion as they returned from captivity:

WHEN THE LORD brought back the captive ones of Zion, We were like those who dream. Then our mouth was filled with laughter, And our tongue with joyful shouting; Then they said among the nations, 'the Lord has done great things for them.' The Lord has done great things for us; We are glad.

RESTORE OUR CAPTIVITY, O Lord, As the streams in the South. Those who sow in tears shall reap with joyful shouting. He who goes to and fro weeping, carrying his bag of seed, Shall indeed come again with a shout of joy, bringing his sheaves with him.

JOY IS an outward manifestation of a thankful heart. Can't you picture the thankful Israelites shouting and rejoicing in what the Lord had done for them? They had suffered for years in captivity and enslavement. When the Lord brought them back to the land it was so far beyond anything they could have imagined, that their only response was joy. That joy resulted in God being recognized by every nation. In other words, their exuberant joy brought glory to God!

It's easy to be thankful when things go our way. It's easy to spread our thankfulness abroad when circumstances are favorable. However, when we are in our moments of weeping and sorrow, do we remember that *those who go to and fro weeping ... shall again return with a shout of joy*? Though at times our daily travails of obediently sowing seeds of thanksgiving can seem sorrowful, in the Lord's timing, we shall reap a bountiful harvest of joy.

PERSONAL APPLICATION:

- Thoughts to ponder: Are you generous? Would your friends and family characterize you as someone with a generous heart? Generosity is about so much more than just money. We can be generous with our time, our words, our praise, or our availability. Record five ways that you can more effectively demonstrate the obedience of generosity.
- It's so easy to grumble and complain! Thankfulness is the antidote to complaining. Take out a blank sheet of paper. (No ... This isn't a quiz!) Each day this week make a list of 10 things for which you are thankful. *Stretch your mind and don't just list the same 10 things over and over each day!!* At the end of the week, tuck that

list in your Bible as a handy reference when
thankfulness is in short supply.

- It's another week, so that means another memory
  verse. Don't forget to review, review, review those
  previous verses!

THE ODD COUPLE

Upon God's faithfulness rests our whole hope of future blessedness. Only as He is faithful will His covenants stand and His promises by honored. Only as we have complete assurance that He is faithful may we live in peace and look forward to the life to come. –A. W. Tozer

While the last four chapters outlined many areas of obedience that we must embrace in order to experience the fullness of joy that the Lord provides for us, the last chapters of the book will take us on a journey through the *residences of joy*. These residing places of joy will become our safe haven, a sanctuary to which we can run in times of need. However, before we get there, it's time to spend a few chapters addressing the elephant in the room ...

If I were you, right about now I'd want to grab my shoulders, shake me mercilessly, and say, "I Get It! Joy can be mine; God promises me joy; but why do I feel so lousy???"

My intention in sharing these Biblical truths about joy has never been to heap a load of guilt on your shoulders. I don't want to add to the burden of already-burdened hearts. However, like those law enforcement officers from Chapter One needed to study the real deal currency in order to recognize the counterfeit, before we begin to look at the counterfeit reality of this world, it was just as necessary for us to study the real deal joy that comes from God. Understanding our role in obedience will give us the weapons we need to win the battle against the enemies of our joy. But now it's time to answer that question: If joy is my possession, why am I unhappy?

Do you remember the old television show, *The Odd Couple*? Fastidious Felix and Messy Oscar attempted to cohabitate peacefully despite their obviously different approaches to daily life. Joy and unhappiness are a lot like Oscar and Felix. Looking in from the outside, we would shake our heads and think to ourselves, "Who in the world thought it was a good idea for those two to become roommates?"

This is probably just my warped *structure-loving* brain, but I even picture joy and unhappiness like Felix and Oscar. In my mind, joy is tidy. Joy provides peace and security because it's uncluttered. The very nature of joy is dusted, organized, and well … joyful! Unhappiness, on the other hand, is just a mess. I assume that unhappiness throws its wet towel on the floor. It leaves dishes in the sink. I'm convinced that unhappiness never, ever, ever makes its bed! (But I digress …)

I think the reason we struggle so much with the reality of unhappiness and balk at the idea that it could be a part of our Christian lives is we are seeing unhappiness as something that it really is not. Just as there is a difference between joy and happiness, unhappiness does not mean joylessness. Being unhappy doesn't mean we're not a *good* Christian, and it certainly doesn't mean that we are sinning! Just looking at unhappiness from the outside can sometimes lead us to assume that it is joylessness, but we have to know exactly what we're looking at in order to truly identify it. Sometimes, just because something *looks like* a familiar object doesn't mean it *is* that familiar object ...

Anyone who knows me well, knows that I'm somewhat of a practical joker. Ok, ok! Not *somewhat*. I AM a practical joker. My poor kids have, on more than one occasion and as the victim of one of my practical jokes, exclaimed, "What kind of mother even does that!!" Uhm... this kind of mother. I have the dubious distinction of being the one who taught my kids to short-sheet beds. I'm notorious for hiding around corners to scare my husband. You don't even want to know about the time I put chicken bouillon cubes in all of my dormitory's shower heads.

Which brings me to Molly's strep test. My third daughter, Molly, spent most of her childhood either contracting, suffering with, or recovering from strep. She was the only child that got to have her own room–simply because she was always contagious. Her dad called her Typhoid Molly. On one of our many trips to the pediatrician, the doctor gave Molly a new type of strep test. This new test looked EXACTLY like a pregnancy test. Of course, it came back positive with a bright red + and my mind began to concoct an evil plan ...

That night, we were scheduled to have dinner with certain members of my family who were quite concerned about the large size of our family. With each new birth announcement, we received a new lecture about my health, over-population, and the neglect that children in large fami-

lies must endure. (To be honest, I'm not sure which child
they would have wanted me to Return to Sender ...) At that
time, we had six children, and I know they were hoping that
Six Was Enough.

When we arrived at their home for dinner, I told them
that we had something serious to tell them. Then, I pulled
out the positive strep test. Their shock and consternation
were a sight to behold. I can hardly express my–quite unbiblical–joy in tricking them into thinking there was another
baby on the way. I know, I know it wasn't very kind of me,
but boy-oh-boy was it satisfying!

They fell for my practical joke because the strep test
looked so convincingly like a pregnancy test. They were
tricked. Unhappiness is a trickster, as well. But it isn't a
sweet, endearing, no-harm-done practical joker like me. No.
Unhappiness is a hurtful bully. Unhappiness tricks us into
believing that because our circumstances have caused our
hearts to be heavy, we have failed in our assignment to live
the *Victorious Christian Life.* Unhappiness throws accusations
at us: Loser, Failure, Sinner, and sometimes, it even causes
us to question our standing before God. Unhappiness
convinces us that any joy that we previously experienced
was probably just a fluke, and we shouldn't expect to have
any joy like that in the future. Unhappiness masquerades as
something that it isn't.

Unhappiness clouds our vision and convinces us that it
is the same thing as joylessness. Let me say this loudly and
clearly: Joylessness and Unhappiness are not the same
thing!! If that were the case, our joy would be based on our
circumstances. But, it's not. That's why the earlier chapters
of this book were so important. We have to know, in the
deepest part of our hearts, that our joy is a gift from God
and is secured forever by our salvation. We must accept,

even when it seems impossible to believe, that God's promises are for our good. We must refuse to allow unhappiness to masquerade as joylessness. Unhappiness is hard enough to deal with ... we mustn't give it more power and authority.

Unhappiness comes in all shapes and sizes. Later in the book, we'll be looking at James 1:2–7, but for now, I want to just pull one verse out of that passage. James 1:2 teaches this truth:

CONSIDER IT ALL JOY, *my brethren, when you encounter various trials.*

THAT WORD *various* is quite an interesting word. It literally means *multi-colored*. According to James, our trials are unique. No trial looks exactly like any other trial that we've experienced. Corporately, our trials are distinctive from every other believer's trials. Remembering this truth will help us to be more compassionate to others, when the trial causing them such unhappiness seems somewhat trivial to us. Jesus doesn't treat our unhappiness as inconsequential! He cares as deeply about your trials as He does about mine. In fact, for each of us, the promise of Matthew 10:29–30 is a precious reminder that we are *of great value* to our Lord. Our value isn't somehow based on our age, or ethnicity, or status, or resume of faithful service. Instead, it is based on our relationship with Christ alone.

The unhappiness of a child is just as valid and painful as the unhappiness of an adult. When our son Peter was three-years old, we planned his birthday party. He was so excited to invite six of his buddies over to play games and share his birthday cake. Sadly, for a variety of unforeseeable reasons, NOONE came to the party. We have a pitiful, albeit hilarious video of poor little Peter sitting alone at the head of a long table set with party plates and favors. While blowing out his birthday candles, he sang a sad, sad rendition of *Happy Birthday to Me*. He can laugh about it now, but his unhappiness at that moment and in the days that followed was crushing to his little heart. We helped Peter as he took his heartache to the Lord. In his own childlike way, he honestly poured out his hurt and disappointment. It was a privilege to help Peter learn how to accept the Lord's compassionate care and to move beyond that hurtful situation.

Fast forward 22 years. Peter and his dear wife Rochelle were expecting their first baby, our first granddaughter. Rochelle's labor was progressing slowly, and the doctors sent her home to labor in her own bed. Heartbreakingly, while she was at home, little Alexis died in her womb. For all of us, and especially Peter and Rochelle, the pain of loss was sudden and felt overwhelming. Peter was devastated and his heart was again crushed with unhappiness.

Same child, but oh such a bigger–in our way of thinking–weight of heart-crushing pain. But for Jesus, the unhappiness of the birthday party was just as important as the unhappiness caused by Alexis' stillbirth. His concern was the well-being of His precious child Peter. The gentle and compassionate care of Jesus was just the same as it had been when Peter was three-years-old. As Peter poured out his hurt and disappointment in prayer, Jesus ministered peace, strength, and joy to our now-adult son. We marveled as we watched the joy of the Lord truly become the strength that upheld Peter and Rochelle through the funeral and the long days following the death of their much-anticipated baby.

There is no Big unhappiness or Small unhappiness in the economy of our Lord. He sees our hurting hearts, and He ministers the medicine of grace and peace to our wounds. He doesn't judge our unhappiness to determine whether or not it's worthy of His attention. He doesn't condemn us for our unhappiness or chide us for struggling to hold on to joy. In fact, He not only acknowledges that we will face unhappy times, but He tells us to expect them. John 16:33 will be in red if you have a red-letter Bible because these are the very words of our Lord:

THESE THINGS I have spoken to you, that in Me you may have peace. In the world you have tribulation, but take courage; I have overcome the world.

JESUS DOESN'T DISREGARD or discount our hurts and unhappiness. But, He also doesn't leave us to wallow in those negative emotions. Instead, after warning us to expect tribulations in our day-to-day living, He reminds us that those tribulations are *no match* for Him. Knowing that Jesus has overcome the world and all of the unhappiness that the world's reality holds for us is what we need in order to face our trials courageously and with peace in our hearts. Understanding that truth certainly doesn't shield us from every trial, but it does mean that we can have confidence in the final outcome of our hardships. As my husband so often reminds me, "I've read the end of the Book ... Jesus wins!

Consider the words of Andrew Murray:

"ALL AROUND YOU *there is a world of sin and sorrow, and Satan is there. But remember, Christ is on the throne; Christ is stronger; Christ has conquered; and Christ will conquer. But wait on God ... Get linked to God. Adore and trust Him as the omnipotent One, not only for your own life, but for all the souls that are entrusted to you. Never pray without adoring His omnipotence ... and the answer to the prayer will Come. Like Abraham you will become strong in faith, giving glory to God, because you account Him who has promised able to perform.*"

ALL THROUGHOUT THE Scriptures are examples of men and women of God who faced dark and unhappy times, yet they still rested on the promise of God's joy. As we consider these specific Bible characters, remember that they don't represent made-up stories or just allegorical examples to teach a lesson. These were real people with real heart hurts, just like us. They suffered loss, and sorrow, and exhaustion, and misunderstanding, but through those trials they learned the discipline of trusting God for their joy. Their lessons are our model as we walk through similar trials.

King David suffered times of unhappy trials. When the Prophet Samuel came to David's father seeking the man who would be King, no one even called David in from the fields and from tending the sheep. Can you imagine the hurt that caused in a young man's heart? When David became a successful warrior in the service of King Saul, his faithful actions were rewarded by Saul's attempts to take his life. I'm sure he felt misunderstood and unappreciated. Have you ever been there?... I sure have. David was forced to flee for his life when his son tried to usurp his throne. He lost a child because of his own sin. His wife laughed at him when he un-self-consciously danced before the Lord. Quite honestly, the list of excuses that would have given David reason to abandon all joy is endless. But over and over in the Psalms, as David pours out his hurt and bitterness to the Lord, his sorrow is turned to joy and his grief is transformed by thanksgiving and praise. Read Psalm 3, or 4, or 5, or 7 or ...The list goes on and on. David knew, as his words teach us, that despite his difficult circumstances, his joy was secure in the Lord.

In Chapter 9 of the Book of Acts, Saul was blinded on the road to Damascus which led to him becoming a Christian. From being one of the chief persecutors of the new Church, Saul was marvelously changed by his encounter with the Lord into a faithful follower of Christ. In Acts 9:20, almost immediately after his conversion, Paul began to proclaim Christ to anyone and everyone who would listen. Can't you picture him bubbling over with the joy of his salvation? He had been changed from an angry, vindictive persecutor into a joyful proclaimer of truth. Unfortunately, that proclamation of truth so angered the religious leaders that he was forced to *escape from Damascus through an opening in the wall while hidden in a large basket.* (Acts 9:25)

I have no doubt that Paul was discouraged. He was sharing the greatest truth that men could ever hear, and yet he had to run for his life. But, this same apostle became the penman of these Scriptures: *More than that, we rejoice in our sufferings,* (Romans 5:3) *rejoice in hope; be patient in tribulation,* (Romans 12:12) *I rejoice in my sufferings for your sake,* (Colossians 1:24) and *Rejoice in the Lord always; again, I will say rejoice!* (Philippians 4:4) Paul, who had experienced the unhappiness that the realities of life in a fallen world bring, still clung to the over-arching theme of his life ... *JOY.*

I want to look at another Biblical character as we continue this discussion of how joy and unhappiness can co-exist in the life of the believer. Just this past Sunday, as I was right in the middle of finishing the final draft of this book, our pastor shared an illustration that really hit home. It was Mother's Day and he was talking about Mary, the Lord's mother. Let's consider two separate passages as we look at her life, and the progression of joy, and unhappiness, and then joy again that she experienced in her role as the mother of Jesus:

AND MARY SAID, "My soul exalts the Lord, and my spirit has rejoiced in God my Savior."–Luke 1:46–47

AND SIMEON BLESSED, and said to Mary His Mother, "Behold, this Child is appointed for the fall and rise of many in Israel, and for a sign to be opposed–and a sword will pierce even your own soul–to the end that thoughts from many hearts will be revealed. –Luke 2:34–35

IN TWO CHAPTERS, Mary is given both a message that caused her to rejoice and a warning that, I'm sure, caused questions and fear in her heart. Eight days after giving birth to the Child that she knew without a doubt came from God, she was delivered a message of pain and sorrow. Can you imagine the confusion she felt in that moment?

In Luke 1, Mary received a message from the angel announcing that she, a virgin, would become the mother to the Son of the Most High. (vs. 32) As a devout Jew, Mary certainly knew and had probably even memorized the prophecies concerning the coming Messiah. As a faithful Jew, she would have been looking and longing for His appearing. Verses 46–55 contain the outpouring of Mary's heart as she considered the great and mighty act that God was working through her life. In verse 47, Mary proclaims her rejoicing in *God her Savior*.

Notice, she isn't rejoicing in the Father; Mary is exalting in the joy of carrying her Savior in her womb. Her knowledge of the ancient texts and prophecies would have made it clear to her that this baby was so much more than just an infant ... He was the One who had been sent by God to rescue Mary and her people! I'm sure the joy of that understanding helped her to walk through the long months of judgment, misunderstanding, and the physical pain of her pregnancy.

Then came the birth of Christ. In Luke Chapter 2, we find Mary and Joseph at the temple with their now eight-day-old baby. The joyful promise that Mary carried in her womb had now become the joyful fulfillment of the baby in her arms. Into this context, righteous Simeon, filled with the Holy Spirit, handed Mary a heavy burden of unhappiness that she would carry for the next thirty-three years.

Luke 2:19 remarks on the fact that Mary *treasured up all these things, pondering them in her heart*. There's no doubt that Simeon's troubling prophecy must have churned over and over in her heart and mind. What could it mean? As a Jew, Mary's understanding of the coming Messiah was that He would be a mighty ruler. He would set His people, the Jews, free. He would have dominion and authority. She could never have imagined that first He would be crucified, and that the freedom He would provide would be freedom from her sin.

For thirty-three years co-mingled with Mary's joy, there was the certain knowledge that her *soul would be pierced*. I'm sure she questioned what that meant. For thirty-three years, a troubling cloud of uncertainty and doubt must have hovered on the edge of the joy she found as Jesus' mother. Jesus always carefully and respectfully cared for Mary. While hanging on the cross, Jesus even delegated the responsibility for her care to His disciple John. But as He grew, Jesus' primary loyalty was no longer to his mother and earthly family. Instead, He aligned Himself with his Heavenly Father. I can imagine that watching Him make that transition brought fear and concern to the heart of His mother ... Was this radical realignment what would bring about the sword that would pierce her soul?

Mary stood at the foot of the cross as her precious son hung dying. She watched Him mocked and shamed. She saw His wounded body. She witnessed His death. In that moment, where was the joy of the angel's birth announcement? Even as a mother myself, I doubt that I can clearly picture Mary's sorrow, hurt, anger, bitterness, fear, and grief. Truly, her joy had been hidden far away, darkened by the fulfillment of Simeon's prophecy.

But then ... Acts Chapter One provides us with the last Biblical account of the life of Mary. In Acts One, the resurrection had already occurred, and Jesus had already ascended into heaven. Acts 1:12–14 records the actions of Christ's followers after His departure. The disciples returned to Jerusalem and gathered together in an upper room where they waited for the arrival of the promised Holy Spirit. But they weren't alone in that upper room. See who joined them in their anticipation:

THESE ALL WITH *one mind were continually devoting themselves to prayer, along with the women, and Mary the mother of Jesus, and with His brothers. –Acts 1:14*

. . .

THERE IN THE UPPER ROOM, Mary joined the disciples in joyful anticipation of the coming Holy Spirit. Finally, the angel's announcement made sense. She had been right to rejoice in God her Savior, but that salvation was more than she could have ever imagined. She had carried and given birth to the One who would save her from her sins. Imagine the joy she found as she more fully could understand the memories that she had experienced throughout the life of her precious Child and King. Oh, what Joy!

Honestly, the foremost example of this juxtaposition of joy and unhappiness must be our King, the Lord Jesus. Each of the Gospel accounts makes it clear that He experienced times of sorrow and sadness throughout His earthly ministry. However, the apex of that sorrow came on the night of His crucifixion. As He saw His prophecy of Peter's denial fulfilled, how could He have felt anything but betrayal? As the crowds who had just tried to crown Him as King called for His death, how could He have been anything but hurt and wounded? As he suffered intense and ongoing physical pain, how could He have felt anything but broken, deserted, and physically helpless? None of those events came anywhere close to being joyful. However, as Hebrews 12:12 reminds us, Jesus endured all of those painful, unhappy events simply for *the joy set before Him*. He is our greatest and highest example!

As difficult and painful as unhappiness can be, often it is our unhappy moments that truly illuminate the joy of our salvation. The happiness of this world is a shallow substitute for the joy that is ours because of our Savior. The simple truth that *Jesus loves me this I know* is ours to snatch and clutch because of what Christ accomplished on the cross. Unhappy times are the sorrowful reality of this lost and fallen world, but for the Christian, our truest reality is Christ and His gift of eternal joy.

There is no doubt that unhappiness and its other manifestations–sorrow, hurt, disappointment, disillusionment–is our enemy. God's desire for His children is joy, not unhappiness, so our responsibility is to battle those things that give unhappiness access to our lives. In the next chapter, we'll spend time learning to recognize the many costumes that unhappiness dons as it seeks to worm its way into our hearts and lives. However, before we get to the next chapter, I encourage you to take some time to just praise your Savior. Will you practice worship and thanksgiving as actions of obedience to show your Lord how thankful you are for the joy that He promises to you- His co-heir? Before we begin to identify and annihilate those red-flag dangers of unhappiness, let's just linger for a bit in the joy-filled presence of our Lord.

PERSONAL APPLICATION:

- Can you think of other Biblical accounts of men or women who experienced both the security of joy and the hardness of unhappy circumstances? Do some research and record what you learn below.

- Choose a verse or verses to memorize for this week. HINT: Mary's Magnificat in Luke 1: 46–55 would be a beautiful passage to hide in your heart!

RECOGNIZING RED FLAGS OF DANGER

A ll of us know there are varying degrees of adversity. Some is life-shattering, such as the death of a loved one or a permanently disabling injury. At the opposite end of the spectrum are situations that are really no more than temporary nuisances, such as an unexpected visitor dropping by when you are working against a tight deadline. All of these circumstances and events, whether trivial or serious, are intended by God to be means of developing more Christlike character.

–Jerry Bridges

Do you know what I consider the worst part of needing to wear glasses? Losing them! I can't tell you how often I misplace something, but I'm unable to find what I've lost because I need to find my glasses, first. Without my glasses on, I misread messages, misplace clothing articles, and misunderstand the directions on medicine bottles.

When it comes to recognizing and dealing with the red

flags and danger signs of impending unhappiness, we need to permanently affix our *discernment-glasses* to the end of our nose! Generally speaking, unhappiness doesn't just appear out of thin air. For most of us, something or someone triggers the circumstances that cause our unhappiness. The more adept we become at seeing those triggers for what they are–DESTRUCTIVE– the more confidently we will do battle with those enemies of our joy.

For clarity, there are women who struggle with unexpected, unexplainable, and untriggered unhappiness. Whether it's because of hormonal imbalances, unresolved past trauma, or some other unknown cause, their hovering unhappiness is a lifelong struggle. For those of you who deal with this, my heart hurts for you! May I encourage you to seek out Biblical counsel. The Word of God truly does have the hope and help that you so desperately need. Notice please that I said *Biblical* counsel. You need someone who can *accurately handle the Word of God* in order to minister help and hope to your heart. (II Timothy 2:15)

For the rest of us, however, unhappiness is much more circumstantial. Sometimes it's a nasty gift of hurtful words that are handed to us by a family member or friend. Much like the dead bird my Labrador retriever presented to me on my 31st birthday ... I swear that dog hated me, but she thought she was giving me the best of the best. Other times, we make choices that open the door for unhappiness to pry its way into our hearts. Either way, the more quickly we recognize unhappiness traveling toward us, the more quickly we can take up our spiritual weapons and do battle against it.

In my book, The Wise Wife, I spent several chapters discussing the two different types of traps that are found in the Scriptures. One trap is the type of trap that catches us unawares. We don't see it coming, and, therefore, we cannot prepare for its entrapment. The second type of trap is much more obvious to us. It sticks out like a sore thumb. Perhaps it's a trap that we've encountered, or even fallen into, time and time again. While the discussion of traps in The Wise Wife primarily focused on how to avoid being entrapped by our own sin, the same types of traps are waiting to ambush our joy and lock us in circumstantial unhappiness.

All of us have experienced traps that caught us by surprise. Whether it was the sudden loss of a loved one or the unpleasant surprise of an unexpected job loss, those types of traps are the kind that we just can't avoid. Their very suddenness places us into a defensive position. We are forced to react because we simply don't have time to proactively prepare to do battle. At those times, it will be the depth and consistency of our relationship with the Lord that provides protection for our hearts and minds.

However, much more often, we are faced with traps of unhappiness that are able to be clearly seen. Both Proverbs 22:3 and 27:12 reiterate the same cautionary truth about the obvious traps of life.

A PRUDENT MAN sees evil and hides himself, The naïve proceed and pay the penalty.

IN OTHER WORDS, if we want to live wisely, we will learn to recognize the unhappiness danger signs in our lives. We will not get as close to those red flags as possible, but instead, we will hide ourselves. The second half of the verse reminds us that should we choose to toy with or proceed toward unhappiness, we will pay the penalty. The penalty of continuing down the road of situational unhappiness is a loss of peace, a distance in our spiritual relationship with the Lord, and ultimately, an inability to recognize and live out our promised joy.

Some of the red flags of unhappiness are forcibly introduced into our lives by others, but sometimes, we are our own worst enemies. Sometimes we shoot ourselves in the foot! Worst yet, sometimes we damage another believer's joyful living through our careless *Friendly Fire*. Through our words and actions, we can become another Christian's red flag signaling danger. Definitely not a title I'd want to have connected with my character.

We must do better than that. Getting caught up in traps of our own choosing will always lead to damaging consequences. I'm afraid that too often, despite the harm that certain actions or relationships cause to our joyful well-being, we heedlessly continue to cultivate those toxic associations with no regard to the destruction that they are causing in our lives.

Let's consider both types of red flags. (Self-induced and others-generated) Once we are able to recognize the danger signs of impending unhappiness, we will then be able to do battle against them. It definitely isn't enough to just say, *"Hey! Look at that red flag ... bummer, I hope it doesn't affect me."* We need to build a strong offense to defeat the enemy's defense. There is no room for co-existence, cooperation, or surrender to the enemies of joy.

In the next chapter, we'll discuss practical ways to build that strong offense and do battle with the enemies of our joy. In this chapter, however, we're just going to focus on identifying the red flags—the danger signs—that should catch our attention and tell us to Beware. Knowing our enemies is the first step in defeating our enemies.

Satan is the first red flag we need to recognize in our battle against our enemies of joy. If *God is for us*, (Romans 8:31) and if His gift to us is eternal joy, we can be certain that Satan longs to make us forget about that gift. There is no greater weapon in Satan's arsenal than the life of a joyless Christian. The unsaved will roll their eyes and label a blatantly rebellious Christian as a hypocrite. They will disregard and ignore such a person's words. A rebellious Christian will have a useless testimony for the Lord, but the joyless Christian actually does much more damage to the Lord's character and testimony.

Our God is a joyful God! (John 15:11; John 17:13) Consider what Nehemiah 8:10 teaches us about our joyful God:

... FOR THE JOY *of the Lord is your strength.*

JUST A CURSORY READING of this verse would indicate that the joy which we are given by the Lord is what strengthens us. That is true. However, it doesn't go far enough. God is not only the giver of joy, He is the source of joy. The joy which He so freely shares with us is first the joy that He possesses. God can share His joy with us because He is joyful.

Satan hates joy. If God's character is the source and origination of joy, Satan's character is the *origination of lies.* (John 8:44) Unlike Jesus, who came to give us *abundant life*, Satan came only to *steal, kill, and destroy.* (John 10:10) From the earliest days in the garden, Satan attempted to call God's words and promises into question. As he said to Eve then, he repeats to us now, *"Did God really say?"* (Genesis 3:1) If he can convince us that God's promises are untrue, he can convince us that we have no right to experience God-given joy. Ephesians 6:11–16 and I Peter 5:8–9 remind us that we are called to engage in all-out, no holds barred *warfare* when it comes to battling Satan and his lies.

Satan is called the *accuser of the brethren*. (Revelation 12:10) The red flags of his accusations tempt us to forget the reality of our God-given joy. He uses statements like: *And you call yourself a Christian? You blew it again!* or *This is it; you can't hope for anything better!* His battle plan is to fill our hearts with despair and to snuff out our testimonies of joy. When he can convince the unsaved that our lives are just as joyless and hopeless as theirs, he has won another major battle for the heart of the unbeliever.

There are other enemies of our joy. Other red flags that we simply can't avoid. Perhaps it's an employer who delights in pointing out our failures. Maybe it's a relative who continually puts us in our place. Possibly our spouse or our children are critical or sarcastic, and their hurtful comments wound our hearts. Sometimes, the circumstances in which we find ourselves are just not conducive to remembering our joy. Biblical counselor and author Ed Welch has this to say about the joy-quenching relationships we encounter:

PEOPLE CAN BE ENEMIES. *They can be consistently against us. They can plot our destruction and be committed to shaming and disgracing us.*

NOPE, you're not crazy! There truly are relationships that don't want anything good for us ... including any joy. There is a Biblical way to handle these relationships, and I promise we'll get there soon. Until then, here's an encouraging Scripture to hold on to for support:

NO TEMPTATION HAS OVERTAKEN you but such as is common to man; and God is faithful, who will not allow you to be tempted beyond what you are able, but with the temptation will provide the way of escape also, that you may be able to endure it. —I Corinthians 10:13

YES, people can make life hard and joy elusive. But, our gracious God has provided ways for us to live joyfully and successfully in the midst of those hard relationships and circumstances. Here's a hint: We can be used as His ambassadors in even the prickliest person's life.

These next few red flags, the ones we can and should avoid, may seem a bit intrusive. You may feel as though I'm meddling in your business. In fact, all of your *who-does-she-think-she-is* defense mechanisms may shift into high gear. That's ok! Sometimes we need another person to come alongside of us to shine a bit of light on our blind spots. My goal is not to make you feel guilty. (Well, maybe a little guilty☺) However, conviction is another matter. IF the Lord convicts you about one of these red flags, please *Stop What You are Doing. Put down the book, Get out your Bible, and Spend some time getting things right with your God!*

Wait a minute ... Do we really know the difference between guilt and conviction? It's vitally important that we understand the difference between the two. Guilt is what Satan loves to bring into our lives. Sometimes he uses our moms, or our friends, or something we read in a book to convince us that we are less than what we should be as

Christian women. He wants us to feel like failures because if that's how we feel, our actions will follow our feelings. Again, he wants us to be ineffective witnesses for Jesus, and trust me when you feel guilty, you'll have no joy and no clear testimony.

Conviction, on the other hand, comes from the Lord and is based in His Word. Often, I read a verse that I've read a hundred times before, and suddenly, this time it convicts my heart and calls me to change. Guilt binds our hearts and convinces us that we'll never be any different than we are now ... It tells us we're stuck. We'll never change. Conviction does just the opposite. It frees our hearts and helps us to find the put-off/put-on path to Biblical growth and change.

Honestly, I hope you'll feel some conviction as we consider these next danger signs. I hope you'll make changes in your life as God brings His conviction to bear on your heart. Why do I say that? Remember, one of the ministries I fulfill is in the role of a counselor. I have spent hours sitting across the table from deeply discouraged women who are struggling to find their joy. As I've listened to them share the habits of their lives, I've too often heard them recount their multiple walks down roads that they knew would lead to heartache and unhappiness. Their unwillingness to see the red flags of danger and to avoid those flags has trapped them in destructive cycles of bitter unhappiness. Their own choices have hidden their joy. Sometimes, we are our own worst enemies.

That's why I hope you DO experience conviction. I've heard their heart-cries, and I know my own tendency to wander where I don't belong. I can make a fairly certain assumption that you, like them and like me, need the Lord's conviction to change. Whether it's laziness, or fear, or hesitation to *rock the boat*, refusing to hide ourselves

from recognizable traps of unhappiness is a willful decision. When we make that decision, we obstinately quench
our God-given joy and rob the Lord of the glory that He
is due.

Busyness is a trap. Busyness is a Huge Red Flag. Let me
say that again with emphasis ... BUSYNESS IS A TRAP! As
we run here and there, filling our days and our calendars
with activities, and meetings, and sports, and the list goes on
and on, we can easily lose sight of joy. Exhaustion is the
natural enemy of joy. When we are over-tired, we are easily
discouraged. I think of Elijah after he killed all of the
prophets of Baal. Exhausted from his ordeal and fearful for
his life, the prophet sat down under a juniper tree and just
wanted to die. Elijah had just performed a great act in the
name of the Lord, but his exhaustion clouded his thinking.
He had no joy in the victory, but only longed to lay down
and die.

Exhaustion will do the same thing to us. It's so easy
when we have no margins in our lives to lose sight of joy in
the midst of going, going, going. The past six weeks have
been a strange time for our country. The Covid-19 pandemic
has forced all of us to slow down and stay home. I've heard
sweet testimonies of family relationships rejuvenated and
neighbors helping neighbors. In spite of the enforced slow-
down, there have been so many positive outcomes. One of
those positive outcomes has been the ability to rest and
refuel. Don't get me wrong; I miss going out to dinner and
the freedom to shop whenever and wherever I want.
However, slowing down has allowed me to catch up on
much-needed sleep. I'm not in a drowsy fog anymore.
Increased energy and a sharper focus have helped me to be
more aware of just how sweetly the Lord has provided for
us. His lovingkindess, in spite of the uncertainty

surrounding Steve's job as an airline pilot, has helped us all to continue to live joyfully.

What do your days and weeks look like on a regular basis? Are you running here and there with no time to slow down and revel in your God-given joy? Or, are you carefully carving out parameters of rest, so busyness doesn't become a battleground with exhausted unhappiness, the opposing General in the war for your joy?

Another red flag that is our own personal responsibility is the red flag of friendships. Look, I understand how important friendships are for our well-being, but any friendship that lures us to walk outside the parameters of God's Word will only end up hurting us. When every time spent together culminates in a weight of conviction on our shoulders, we can't help but miss out on joy. When we walk away from our encounters regretting things we said or activities in which we participated, we can count on being unhappy. Conviction over poor choices and regret do nothing to build and preserve our joy.

I shared earlier about how difficult it was for me to walk away from a destructive friendship. Let me reiterate, when a friendship leads us away from faithful adherence to the Word of God, we are responsible for our own lack of joy! That does not mean that every friendship that has a *we blew it* moment needs to end. Often, as the Lord is convicting us about poor choices in a friendship, He is convicting our friends, as well. That conviction can and should turn into God-honoring change.

The next danger zone is our personal choices and daily habits. These can become red flags that alert us to the danger of unhappiness and joyless living. What kind of personal choices fall into this category? I would include things we read, whether on paper or the internet, places we go, and the possessions we covet. All of these things have the potential to distract us from joy and leave us wallowing in feelings of unhappiness.

What goes in through our eyes will certainly affect our hearts. When it comes to the books and magazines that we read, a good measurement of acceptability for us is the little saying *If there's any doubt; there's no doubt.* If we are going to invest our precious time in reading something, the Scriptures makes it clear that we must be *fully convinced in our own mind* (Romans 14:5) that what we are ingesting is not damaging to us. That means that there may be certain books or publications that are fine for you but bring darkness into my life. Anything that distracts me from Biblical living will cause spiritual unhappiness. Spiritual unhappiness blocks me from seeing the joy that God has provided for me! It does the same for you ...

This is somewhat of a sacred cow, but how do you invest your time online? The Internet, itself, is morally neutral. However, there are sites and destinations on the Internet that will cause spiritual harm to us! Sometimes, it isn't so much the destination, as it is the time we spend there. If we are lingering on a Social Media site and filling our hearts with critical or cynical political commentary, there is no doubt that we're going to struggle to cling to joy. If we are staying up late comparing our lives to the Pinterest perfect lives on the Internet, we will be tempted to become discontent, not exactly conducive soil for the growth of joy.

I consider social media temptations our own personal red flags because only you–and the Lord–can determine whether your time spend online is producing joy or one of the many facets of unhappiness. Please, *be hard on yourself* as you evaluate your choices in this area! We tend to judge how much time our friends, sisters, or children spend on social media while rationalizing our own wasted hours. Jeremiah 17:9 reminds us that *our hearts are deceitful*. If there is any doubt in your mind about the stewardship of your time on social media ... there's no doubt that you need to make some changes! Multiple studies have shown that social media addiction, (Yes, let's call it what it is.) can be just as difficult to combat as alcohol or drug addiction. You may have to wean yourself slowly from the sites that steal your time and attention, but the joy you'll recover will be well worth the battle!

The places that we go can become danger signs for us in the battle to preserve our joy. For me, some of my old college haunts bring up memories that are just too tempting. It's not that I'm fearful of succumbing to the same unbiblical temptations, but the memories of my sinful pursuits lose their horror, and I once again begin to see them as *harmless fun*. Any place that threatens our joy must become an off-limit destination. Remember, the Proverb doesn't say that we are to build up an immunity to danger, or train ourselves to walk closely to the danger zone. Rather, we are to *hide ourselves*. I Timothy 6:11 uses the forceful word *flee* to warn us from lingering in harm's way.

Some of the unhappiest women that I have met have also been some of the most discontent. When we feel as though we've somehow gotten the short end of the stick, or if we think that we deserve more than we have, we will find our joy-lenses clouded with unhappiness. This lack of contentment definitely shows up in our attitude toward *stuff*. Our culture does nothing to help us to be joyful with what we have! Advertisements, and commercials, and billboards all flaunt the next best thing that would make our lives complete! Although these tempting ads may hold some culpability in our temptation to succumb to discontentment, the choice to continue down the road of disappointment and displeasure is ours alone.

However, there's a different type of discontent that I believe is even more harmful not only to our joy, but more importantly, to our ability to glorify God. Consider with me for a moment, I Timothy 6:6. I really like how the NIV translates this particular verse:

BUT GODLINESS *with contentment is great gain.*

IN OTHER WORDS, living a life of godliness, coupled with contentment, will bring us great blessing, *or gain*. The idea of gain in this verse is the concept of a large or wonderful advantage. Those who live godly will possess the advantage of a spiritual life that will uphold them throughout all of life's difficulties.

But now, for a moment, let's consider the converse of this passage. Here's where I think spiritual discontent enters the picture and mars our joyful living. If we flip the verse around, the contrast would look like this:

GODLINESS WITHOUT CONTENTMENT IS ..._____.

I THINK the answer to fill-in-the-blank is the word *legalism*. When we perform our righteous acts simply because it's what we are told we must do, or so others will see them, or so we're just a little more spiritual than anyone else, or because that's what we've always done ... there will be no gain, no advantage, and only discontent.

Legalism breeds unhappiness. Legalism crushes all of the joy out of the life of the believer and replaces it with Pharisaical self-righteousness. Legalism destroys God's gift of joy! Besides squeezing all of the joy out of us, legalism heaps a burden of works-focused, grace-neglecting rules and regulations on the backs of others.

We must seek to walk godly before our Lord. However, true godliness comes from a heart and life that has been changed through its interaction with the Living God. It never comes from a rule book! The Bible is a book of abundant life, not a manual of rules for *gnat-straining* perfectionism. (Matthew 23:24)

Another red flag deserves our attention, and that is the red flag of worry. It isn't that worry squeezes out our joy like legalism does, but worry can so block our vision that we can't even glimpse joy through the worry-clouds of life. Worry most often takes the form of fear, (specific worry) or anxiety (generalized worry). I even know women who worry about how often they get worried! Believe it or not, there are 366 commands in the Bible to *Fear Not*. Obviously, God knew man would have a propensity to worry, so He gave us a worry-squashing command for each day of the year and one extra for leap year.

Worry is so counter-productive because it is based on the unknown. Worry is a focus on the what-ifs of life. What if my child gets sick? What if I lose my job? What if I never find "The" one? What if I let them down? You see, none of those what-ifs are answerable because they aren't founded in reality. Let's look at these encouraging words from II Corinthians 9:8:

. . .

AND GOD IS able to make all grace abound to you, that always having all sufficiency in everything, you may have an abundance for every good deed.

WHEN WE ARE IN NEED, God will absolutely give us the grace we need to bear up under the reality of our trials. In fact, He will give us abounding grace so we may have an abundance for every good deed. However, God does not promise to give us grace for our reckless what-if thoughts. In fact, the Scripture calls those types of thoughts *vain imaginations*, and we are commanded to *take them captive and make them obedient to Christ*. (II Corinthians 10:5) For God to pour out grace for our vain imaginations would be a waste of His priceless gift of grace.

When we worry, we're really just living out that good, old-fashioned concept of fretting. The dictionary defines fretting in two ways, both applicable to our actions of worry. The first definition of fretting is *to be constantly and visibly anxious or worried*. Our fretting does harm to more than just us. When we are visibly anxious, we will pass on that anxiousness to everyone around us. In a family unit, that type of constant worry will erode security and cause havoc in relationships.

The second definition of fretting is perhaps an even more appropriate way to describe our worry. It is *to gradually wear away at something by rubbing or gnawing*. That's such a visual picture of our worry! Worry will wear away our ability to experience joy.

I have two little Goldendoodle puppies. (Daisy and Dixie) When I give my spoiled babies a new blanket, they both continually gnaw on the corner of their blanket. They fuss and fret and chew until the edge is worn and frayed.

Then, as their very over-indulgent owner, I go get them a new blanket. That's how we act with our worries; we gnaw on them, we replay the worst-case scenario over and over in our mind, we imagine the most awful outcomes, and ultimately ... we lose sight of any joy!! There is an inevitable consequence of worrying and that consequence is unhappiness.

This final red flag may seem totally obvious, but I'd be remiss if we didn't mention it in this chapter. Willful, unconfessed sin will cloud our joy and damage our intimacy with the Lord. Although we all sin and will continue to do so until the day we go to be with Christ, willful sin falls into an especially disruptive category. Willful sin is an active choice to disregard the commands of the Lord and to purposefully *walk in darkness*. (I John 1:6)

There's a Biblical remedy for willful, unconfessed sin. There's a Biblical remedy for worry, and exhaustion, and Satan, and every other red flag that waves its dangerous signal to us. Won't you spend some time thinking over and praying about these red flags? If we are to battle victoriously, we must know our enemy. Learning about our enemy will help us to recognize the enemy's shortcomings, as well as realizing our own weaknesses. When we know our weaknesses, we can prayerfully strengthen ourselves in order to contend with our foes. The battle surely belongs to the Lord, but as His faithful foot soldiers, we must be prepared to engage the enemy wisely if we are going to win the war and protect our joy!

PERSONAL APPLICATION:

- Consider your own personal enemies in the war for joy. Is there any particular enemy that you already know is just aching to engage you in battle? Record that enemy in the space below, and find 5 Scriptures that will help you as you become battle-ready.

- Gratitude is the antidote to discontent! In the spaces below, record five things for which you are grateful. If they are blessings that you've received from someone else, (i.e. possessions, encouragement, teaching) write a note of thanks to that person.

- Choose one of the five verses that you just looked up and commit it to memory!

ARMED FOR BATTLE

If our life with Christ is right, all will come out right. Instruction and suggestion and help and training in the different departments of the work may be needed; all that has value. But in the long run, the greatest essential is to have the full life in Christ—in other words, to have Christ in us, working through us. – Andrew Murray

This sin-stained world is a treacherous place! The ruler of this world has no desire to see you succeed. The culture tempts us and our flesh wars within us. However, we are not left alone in the battle. Our Lord has won the war and He is with us in each and every personal skirmish of the campaign against our joy.

In the last chapter we discussed many, many red flags. For the believer, those red flags must be our call to action. The battle to realize the fullness of our joy in Christ is far too important to ever let down our guard. This chapter is really all about the ministry of the Holy Spirit ... His ministry *to us* through encouragement, exhortation, comfort, or conviction in times of temptation and trial, and His ministry *through us* to other believers when they face those same struggles and hardships.

Whether the red flag of danger comes through sudden and unexpected circumstances, or appears as a result of our own choices, the best defense is a great offense. Behind every Biblical solution to our struggles lies first a foundational and faithful relationship with the Lord. When the red flag is raised and the battle cry sounds, we won't be able to make-up for lost time with the Lord. A prepared soldier is much more likely to be a successful soldier.

When my husband was an officer in the Navy, we faced several nine-month deployments. Preparing for his departure required quite a bit of planning and preparation. We had to update our will. We had to fill out power-of-attorney paperwork. We had to consider anything and everything that could possibly need his attention during the nine-months of his deployment.

For me, the strangest part of the work-up to deployment happened in his squadron. Once they were overseas, the entire squadron had to begin a 12-on/12-off flight and rest time schedule. Instead of days or weekends off, deployment meant around the clock work. About ten days before leaving for each deployment, the squadron, while still at home, would practice their 12-on/12-off schedule. That meant that in the last few days of being home, Steve had to stay in the barracks on base and *practice* being on deployment. It was just such a bizarre concept to me. (And quite honestly, it ticked me off since he was going to be leaving soon, anyway.) We used to joke that they were *preparing to prepare to prepare.*

The first time we went through that cycle, I really didn't understand what the big deal was about all of that preparation. We weren't at war, and it just seemed like a useless waste of time. However, on Steve's second deployment, shortly after he arrived overseas, his crew was called upon to respond to an act of international aggression. All of that pre-work and preparation at home paid off in that moment. They were able to quickly launch the crew and successfully complete their mission. All of the sudden, preparing to prepare to prepare didn't seem like such a silly idea.

Let's move that illustration into our spiritual lives. If we are to do battle against the red flags of sin, and worry, and exhaustion, and Satan, and more ... we must be prepared. If our daily walk with the Lord is characterized by growth and change and joyful obedience, when we are ambushed by a red flag that brings discouragement, we will be ready to defeat it. When joy is a steadfast companion and our sweetest friend, we will be attuned to anything that threatens its position in our lives. There is nothing that will replace a good offense when it comes to preparing ourselves to win the battle for our joy.

If there is a single, Biblical word to describe this spiritual offense, it is the word *Faith*. As we grow in faith, and learn how to walk more obediently because of our faith, our lives will be changed. And not just our *spiritual* lives. Growing in faith will develop our convictions and sharpen our focus. Our actions, words, thoughts, and intentions will become more aligned with the Word of God. When that happens, we won't have any division between our earthly lives and our spiritual lives. At that point, everything we think, say, and do will flow from a deep well of spiritual health. That type of relationship with the Lord will allow joy to take its rightful place in our hearts and minds. Jeremy Pierre, in his book, <u>The Dynamic Heart in Daily Life</u>, puts it like this:

"Faith plugs into the regular functions of the heart—what people think about, the things people want in life, the choices people make—and reroutes their entire day, week, mon, and year. Faith in Jesus reaches into the very soul and transforms one's life. Faith therefore, is lived out in daily life: It is not a Sunday thing. It is not an alternate state of mind people try to enter during a religious service. Faith is dynamically expressed in the way people intuitively respond to their everyday circumstances.

FAITH, therefore, is the inner transformation of the soul that reveals itself through our actions. Faith is the conduit for joy-filled living as a result of our settled relationship with Christ.

So, the basis of a successful offense against the unhappiness that would cloud our joy is faith. Alongside that faith, however, is the necessity of recognizing just how wretched we are when we allow our joy to be clouded and hidden from view. King David described what it's like to regain our joy after wallowing in joylessness when he penned these words in Psalm 34:4–7:

I sought the Lord and He answered me, And delivered me from all my fears. They looked to Him and were radiant, And their faces shall never be ashamed. This poor man cried and the Lord heard him, And saved him out of all his troubles. The angel of the Lord encamps around those who fear Him, And rescues them.

WHEN ONCE WE'VE tasted the joy of our salvation, to find ourselves struggling to regain that joy is truly a frightening thing. Our response to that struggle is the reason for the title of this book. When we begin to sense that our joy is slipping from view, or that our joy is hidden from our sight, our only response should be to snatch hold of our joy and grasp it with tightly gripped fingers of faith. If the joy of the Lord truly is our strength, (Nehemiah 8:10) losing sight of that joy is indeed a fearful thing.

For twenty-six years, our family has gone to Bethany Beach, Delaware, for our yearly family vacation. That vacation is the highlight of my year, and we have so many special memories from Bethany and the nearby town of Rehoboth. Every year without fail, we visit the old-fashioned board-walk amusement park, Funland. We play Skee-ball, smash each other with bumper cars, and most importantly and without fail, we ride the restored carousel. For fifteen years, I had toddlers on that carousel. (Yes, I believe I will receive a special toddler crown when I get to heaven!) Toddlers who, because they were so terribly excited to be on Real Horses– although they were just painted wooden horses–would sometimes forget to grasp the reins. That meant that for fifteen years, I rode the carousel standing up and facing backwards to hold on to my toddlers and make sure they didn't fall off. Now, I get to watch my own children ride what we so fondly refer to as the Vomit Comet, standing up and facing backwards while they keep my precious, adorable– but still distractible–grandchildren safely seated on their wooden steeds.

The highlight of that old-fashioned carousel is the brass ring that dangles temptingly from the ceiling of the ride. When my toddlers would mount their horses, they would excitedly tell me how they were going to be the first to grab the ring. They would yell to their siblings that the ring was going to be theirs! But toddlers have a short attention span. As soon as the music began, they would begin to wave to the bystanders. They would reach down and pat their pony. They would lean over to see what their siblings were doing. They never, ever managed to grab the ring. However, once they got a little older–probably school-aged–that dynamic began to change. Instead of waving, or patting, or spying on anyone else, they were focused on one thing and one thing only–snatching that brass ring. Once they snatched it, they held on for dear life and proudly displayed their victory to the rest of the family.

That's exactly what our response should be to joy! We need to snatch it and hold on to it with a fierce grip of faith! Our knuckles should turn white as we clutch it with the desperation of a child eager to snatch the brass ring. Unfortunately, we're too often exactly like my toddlers. We get distracted. We look at our circumstances, or the things we don't have, or the successful lives that all our friends seem to be living, or our discouragement, and the list just seems to grow. Instead of a relentless focus on snatching the brass ring of joy, we allow ourselves to revolve through life in a continual circle of discouragement and unhappiness, *forgetting that the Brass Ring of Joy is already ours*!

The verb form of the word snatch means *to quickly seize something in a rude or eager way*. When it comes to our God-given joy, there's nothing rude about it! We must snatch, grasp, and cling tightly to our joy. When we don't, our joy will be hidden, and red flags of dangerous unhappiness will go unnoticed and undefeated. Joy will seem elusive, and we'll begin to doubt the promises of God.

How can we do effective battle against Satan's relentless attacks on our joy? Quite honestly, the first step in winning the battle against Satan's attacks is to recognize his weapons of warfare. When we realize that Satan is the enemy of our joy and the accuser of our hearts, his power over us will be weakened. Wise Christian fill their hearts with Scripture to counteract his attacks. Satan doesn't attack us in a one-size-fits-all manner. For some, he tries to convince us that we are failures. For others, his attack comes as a reminder of our past sins. Perhaps one of his greatest weapons is the thought that we are a disappointment to God.

Our third daughter, Molly–yes, Typhoid Molly– joined the Air Force after finishing college. When she arrived at Basic Training, her drill instructor began a relentless campaign to convince little Molly that every failure in her quest to become an enlisted airman was a disappointment to her officer father. Over and over the drill instructor told Molly that her dad was embarrassed by her failures; he was disappointed in her performance, and he probably wished that he wasn't her father.

Of course, we had no idea what was going on. We didn't know what Molly was being told, and her dad certainly wasn't disappointed in her ... just the opposite. He was proud and excited about her achievements. When Molly was finally allowed to call us, she poured out her guilt and sorrow to her dad. Over and over, she begged his forgiveness for failing him as a daughter and embarrassing him as an officer.

Molly was distraught, but her father's wise words brought comfort, consolation, and finally, joy to her heart. He told her just how proud he was of her. He reminded her that he loved her and cherished her regardless of her momentary failures. He repeatedly assured her of her place in his heart and the permanence of his relationship to her as her dad. Molly's heart and hope were restored because her father took the time to heal her wounded emotions. He silenced the lies of her drill instructor with the truth of his relational love.

Our Heavenly Father has done the same for us. His Word is full of affirmations of His love and reminders of the permanence of our relationship with Him. Consider these verses and allow the Word to minister peace and joy to your heart!

See how great a love the Father has bestowed upon us, that we should be called children of God' and such we are ...– I John 3:1

And we have come to know and have believed the love which God has for us. God is love, and the one who abides in love abides in God, and God abides in him. –
I John 4:16

The Lord appeared to him from afar, saying, "I have loved you with an everlasting love; Therefore, I have drawn you with lovingkindness." –Jeremiah 31:3

Give thanks to the God of heaven; His love endures forever. –
Psalm 136:26

But Thou, O Lord, art a God merciful and gracious, slow to anger
and abundant in lovingkindness and truth. —Psalm 86:15

I COULD SPEND weeks and weeks cataloging all that the
Scriptures have to teach about the eternal love of our God
toward us. His Word is our weapon to defeat Satan's lies.
The continual assurance of His love and the permanence of
our relationship with Him can keep our joy intact when
Satan's accusations threaten to shield it from our view. As we
prepare to prepare to prepare for the battle against Satan's
deceptions, our ability to remember God's love will be our
best weapon, and His joy will be our strength.

The short list of verses found above is a good starting
place, but let me challenge you to add to that list each and
every day. Use your concordance–or Google–and find verses
that are specific to the particular lies that Satan uses to
threaten your joy. There is no such thing as too much Scripture when it comes to building an arsenal for spiritual
success. Don't just keep a list of the Scriptures in your Bible,
though. We need quick access to God's reassurance when
our joy is in danger! Write some verses on cards and stick
them in your purse. Place some verse cards on your kitchen
windowsill. Tape them to your bathroom mirror. Trust me,
many mornings when I look in the mirror, I need some
quick reminders of God's unfailing love for a mess like me!

To be honest, sometimes our friends can be messengers
for Satan. I don't think they do so intentionally, but their
words, whether discouraging, sarcastic, or just plain unbiblical, can add sorrow to our already gloomy hearts. Let's cut
Mrs. Job a break right now, (After all, she had just lost her
children and home when she delivered her sad counsel to

Job.) but consider with me the counsel of his three unhelpful friends. In Job, Chapters 4–31, his friends accused him of *doing evil*, *abandoning God*, and then they placed the blame for his suffering directly on his character. Some friends! Whenever I read of their discouraging counsel, the Lord brings to mind, *and such were some of you* ... (I Corinthians 6:11) Although I Corinthians is speaking of specific sins, that *such were some of you* pricks my conscience. I'm afraid that, too often, I have been like Job's friends– an instrument of Satan, used to bring condemnation into the lives of my friends.

In the same way that the Word of God can protect us from Satan's fiery darts of accusation, it will be our protector and defender from the inadvertent–and sometimes, pointedly harsh–discouragement that other Christian's hand to us. Run to His Word. Allow the Scriptures to remind you of the truth regarding *Who* you are and *Whose* you are.

Concerning those other red flags, you know, the ones we hold responsibility for allowing to threaten our joy, one single character quality is the basis of our weaponry. Self-control, as directed by Holy Spirit control, will help us to combat the red flags of busyness, exhaustion, harmful friendships, what we feed on with our eyes and ears, where we stray with our feet, our discontent, and worry. It kind of makes me think of the children's song, "Oh be careful little feet where you go ... Oh be careful little eyes what you see ... Oh be careful little ears what you hear!" However, our lack of self-control over these red flags of danger isn't childlike or cute. According to the Scriptures, it's foolish, and when we behave foolishly, *we will reap the fool's consequences*. (Proverbs 28:26)

Self-control is not a cookie-cutter response in each and every situation. As we seek the guidance of the Holy Spirit,

He will direct our paths. In fact, each believer's obedient and self-controlled response to the guidance of the Spirit will be uniquely different from every other believer's obedient response. The point is that we must choose to be obedient!

Obedience begins by asking the Spirit to reveal any danger signs or red flags that we are ignoring. Then, we must seek the Lord's forgiveness for our willful choices. I'm afraid that sometimes we don't ask because we don't really want to know. Giving up something or someone that brings pleasure to our lives seems so difficult, even when that momentary pleasure later hides our God-given joy. Please remember that God never prompts us to give up something that is spiritually good for us. He only points out those areas in our lives that are detrimental to our relationship with Him and are blocking the joyful life that He longs for us to live.

When I'm grasping something that should instead be abandoned, it's Just. Plain. Exhausting. I'm fairly confident that it's the same for you. In those times of dogged insistence upon having our own way, we're much like King David who felt as though his *body was wasting away*. (Psalm 32:3) There truly is no peace outside of faithful obedience to the Lord. When the Holy Spirit exposes a red flag of danger that is threatening our joy, the only appropriate response is immediate and complete obedience to the Spirit's direction.

We're helped in that obedience as we remember that the Lord is on our side. These are the words of Jesus to us, as recorded in Matthew 11:28–30.

Come to Me, all who are weary and heavy-laden, and I will give you rest. Take my yoke upon you, and learn from Me, for I am

gentle and humble in heart; and you shall find rest for your souls.
For my yoke is easy, and My load is light.

THE WORLD SAYS that submitting our wills, our wishes, and our desires is a heavy burden. But our reality is not the world's reality. For us, abandoning the damaging red flags that threaten our joy and rob us of our peace is the road to rest for our souls. Our Lord is gentle and humble. He longs to replace those temporarily enticing joy-robbing red flags with permanent and faith-building rest, peace, and joy for our souls. As missionary Jim Elliot said before being martyred by members of the Auca Indian tribe in Ecuador, "He is no fool who gives up what he cannot keep, to gain what he cannot lose."

Let's consider a significant red flag that needs special attention as we consider how the Holy Spirit can minister help and hope in the battle to preserve our joy. The Word of God can reassure and strengthen us to stand against Satan and his messengers. Self-control, as directed by the Holy Spirit, can help us to battle our own personal danger signs. However, when it comes to willful, unconfessed sin, we don't need reassurance or self-control; *we need repentance, confession, and restoration with our Lord.*

Habitual sin will build an impenetrable wall between us and our joy. Habitual, unconfessed sin hardens our hearts and makes us blind to our own culpability. The longer we continue in the same sin, the less conviction we will recognize, and the more tenaciously we will cling to our *rights.* The best offense against ever starting down the road of habitual sin is to acknowledge our sin as soon as the Holy Spirit makes us aware that we are sinning.

But what about sin that is already cemented in our hearts? How can we deal with that sin and regain our joy? Thankfully, God has given us the spiritual reset button of forgiveness in order to right our wrong relationship with Him and begin to walk in joy once again. It's not a formula or a difficult process to push the reset button. In fact, it's clearly and simply outlined in I John 1:9:

If we confess our sins, He is faithful and righteous to forgive us
our sins and to cleanse us from all unrighteousness.

YES, it's really that simple. We confess; God forgives. And when God forgives us, we are cleansed from all of that yucky, stubbornly-held-on-to sin that hides our joy and hurts our relationship with Him. Romans 6:4 reminds us that God has provided forgiveness that allows us to *walk in newness of life*. That newness of life is our righteousness as found in Psalm 118:15:

The sound of joyful shouting and salvation is in the tents of the
righteous...

I DON'T KNOW about you, but that's the only tent that I wouldn't mind living in. God's precious possession for His children is joy and nothing, especially our own willful sin, should ever be permitted to separate us from that joy.

So, the Word of God, self-control, and obedient repentance, confession of sin, and restoration with God are the weapons that will ensure victory in the battle to protect our joy. The Holy Spirit is our General and He can provide us with a battle plan that is sure to be victorious. When we put our spiritual weapons into action, we'll develop a winning offense.

There's one more necessary element that will help us in our battle. This isn't just a weapon for the war to protect our joy; it's actually a tool we need on a daily basis. We need this tool clamped around our hearts and minds to help us successfully navigate this ofttimes stinky world in which we live. The tool that I'm talking about is an eternal perspective.

An eternal perspective is just what it sounds like. It is a perspective that is focused on the reality of eternity. An eternal perspective will help to give our circumstances and situations the attention that they deserve, rather than the attention that they demand. An eternal perspective is one of those counter-intuitive ways by which Christians are called to live differently than the world around them.

In this culture, everything is a Big Deal! Whether it's politics, or the latest fad, or who-said-what-about-whom ... Everything becomes a larger than life issue and we are bombarded by the latest, greatest worst-case scenario. Seriously, if we spend any amount of time surfing social media or watching the news, the only proper response would be to run to our bedrooms and hide under the covers.

On the next page, you'll find a literal representation of just how important most of these issues are in light of eternity. Don't freak out, we'll discuss this topic more in the light of the Scriptures.

LOOK FOR IT...

Did you see it? Did you see that teeny-tiny, itty-bitty dot on the page? Now, take a deep breath ... Most of the worries, concerns, issues, circumstances, and situations that crowd our thoughts and threaten our joy are just that big in light of eternity! When considered on the timeline of forever, they are miniscule.

Hear me now ... I did not say that they are inconsequential. Remember, we already observed from the Gospels that Jesus said that what matters to us, matters to Him. However, these issues of life in a fallen world need to be contained within their proper context. They need to be limited to their time-constrained sphere of influence. They need to be ... wait for it ... embraced as the means of bringing us to eternal perfection!

Let's look now at the entirety of James 1:2–8:

Consider it all joy, my brethren, when you encounter various trials, knowing that the testing of your faith produces endurance. And let endurance have its perfect result, that you may be perfect and complete, lacking in nothing. But if any of you lacks wisdom, let him ask of God, who gives to all men generously and without reproach, and it will be given to him. But let him ask in faith without any doubting, for the one who doubts is like the surf of the sea driven and tossed by the wind. For let not that man expect that he will receive anything from the Lord, being a double-minded man, unstable in all his ways.

Allow me to get nerdy for a moment. In the first two verses of this passage, the main independent clause is *count it all joy*. There are two subordinate clauses: *when you encounter various trials* and *knowing that the testing of your faith produces endurance*. The first subordinate clause is <u>temporal</u>, meaning it can't stand on its own. The second is <u>causal</u>, a clause that defines the meaning behind the main clause. Stay with me here ...

The way the verse is translated is a bit clunky in English. A better reading would be: *My brethren, when you encounter various trials, consider it all joy knowing that the testing of your faith produces endurance.* In other words, the trials are not the bearers of joy ... the anticipated end result of endurance is the source of the believer's joy.

I'm afraid that too often, we simply read *Count it all joy when you encounter various trials*, and our brains stop right there. When we do that, we're forced to slap on our *I'm-fine-how-are-you* smiles and simply try to push through our pain. Although our hearts balk at the notion, we try to muscle out the *Good Christian* life by calling our trials joyful and trying to ignore their grievous impact on our lives. Nothing could be further from the truth. Trials aren't joyful; in fact, they STINK!!

However, for the believer, those stinky trials are not the end of the world. We know from the truth of God's Word, that this world is not our home; it's not our final destination! Since this world is not our home, our trials are not our destiny. In Psalm 30:4–5, King David reminds us of this eternal truth:

Sing praise to the Lord, you His godly ones, And give thanks to His holy name. For His anger is but for a moment, His favor is for a lifetime; Weeping may last for the night, But a shout of joy comes in the morning.

Yes, our trials can be devastatingly difficult. We may not see them resolved this week, or this year, or even in this lifetime. However, we have a precious promise of God's favor for a lifetime. His answer to our trial may only come when we go to be with Him, *but it will come!* Do you remember what you read earlier in the book about our circumstances? Our circumstances always have two primary purposes: We are to bring God glory, and He can be trusted to produce good from every situation. When we are tempted to wonder, "What good can come of this?" James 1:2–3 reminds us that one of the *goods* from our circumstances is the production of *endurance* in our spiritual lives.

Let's keep going. When I am faced with the various trials of life, I really just want answers! My mind races with *what if*, and *why me*, and *how is this going to be resolved* questions that keep me awake at night. Verse 5 tells me that God isn't annoyed by my questions. He isn't wondering why I just don't have more faith. He isn't irritated when I come to Him over and over. In fact, He is ready and eager to generously give me the wisdom that I seek in order to glorify Him through the process.

The book of James goes on with an exhortation as we are asking our myriad of questions. You would think that knowing God wants to answer our questions is enough, but James points out a real shortcoming in our response to God's answers. When we begin to receive God's wisdom, we doubt Him. That doubt causes us to be unstable, not just when it comes to the particular trial in which we find ourselves, but as verse 8 points out, we are unstable in ALL our ways.

Perhaps God's answer isn't what we want to hear. Or perhaps His answer brings conviction of sin. Or perhaps the answer is wait, or be still, or trust that this is simply to build endurance. Regardless, when we doubt the wisdom that comes from God, our hard circumstance will be made even more difficult by our topsy-turvy, driven-by-the-wind response.

Our faithless doubting of God's purposes for our trial will only cause us to stare more intently at the trial. I had a pastor years ago who would always remind us to, "Gaze at Christ and just glance at your circumstances." Such good advice, but oh-so-hard to yank my thoughts into submission. The next page shows a literal illustration of what our circumstances become when they consume our thoughts.

FALSE PERSPECTIVE

If you look closely in the center of the circle, you'll see that the reality of our circumstances is still the same in the light of eternity. However, when we fret and turn our situation over and over in our minds, that teeny-tiny spot gets hidden by a false reality. Our circumstances become a new and growing reality. Our trial grows and grows until it almost completely blocks our view of joy. The longer we stare at it, the bigger it becomes. That's when we need to wrestle our gaze away from our trial, no matter how difficult or devastating the situation, and force ourselves to gaze upon the Lord.

Yes, we'll absolutely have to glance back at that trial. But, when our glances are tempered and disciplined by a focused gaze upon Jesus, the trial will lose its power and our eternal perspective will be restored. Instead of appearing to be the only perspective, our Godzilla-sized trial will shrink back down to its proper eternal perspective. Don't get me wrong ... its hard, hard work. Depending upon the severity of our trial, sometimes we just can't wrestle our gaze back to Christ on our own. We have to have help. That's why we need Christian friends who will point us to the Scriptures and remind us of the power of our God to overcome our circumstances.

Really, those Christian friends are another tool in our daily battle to live Christ-honoring and joy-filled lives. This past fall, I was reeling from a family issue that just threatened to overwhelm me. There didn't seem to be any clear way to resolve it Biblically and my heart was aching. To be honest, I really wanted to run to a couple of my Christian friends with whom I knew it would be safe to vent my anger, frustration, fear, and sorrow. They're dear sisters in the Lord and I knew they wouldn't mind if I let 'er rip with my complaints. I also knew that they would commiserate with me. They'd agree with my assessment and be offended on my behalf... So, tempting!

However, deep in my heart, I knew that to go to them was the wrong decision. I didn't need empathy. I didn't need anyone to add to my indignation and hurt. I needed someone who would point me to God's Word and remind me of the truth about my situation. Thankfully, I have a dear sister in Christ who fills that role beautifully. She prayed for me before I arrived and pointed me back to the road of truth and trust. She helped me cast off my fears and focus on how I could bring glory to God ... She helped me to take ownership of my own responsibility to glorify God, regardless of the actions of anyone else involved in the situation.

Ladies, we ALL need friends like that! Not buddies who will just join our pity party or jump on the woe-is-me bandwagon. We need Spirit-filled friends who know their Bibles. We need friends who will encourage us, but who aren't afraid to exhort us and, who sometimes, give us a much-needed kick in the pants. The Bible calls that type of friendship true *fellowship*. It's based on our mutual desire to walk faithfully in the consistent direction of God-glorifying obedience, and it's a far-cry from the pot luck, let's-just-hangout fellowship that we settle for today. Do you have sisters-in-Christ who can fill your need for true fellowship? If not, begin to pray today that God will provide such relationships.

Which brings us to the final section of this chapter. If we need and desire that type of fellowship, we must be prepared to live out that true fellowship for others. True fellowship means that we will love our brothers and sisters in Christ, and part of loving them means recognizing when they are in a battle for joy. Unlike Cain who had no desire to be his *brothers-keeper*, (Genesis 4:9) we must develop a heart of compassion for our brothers and sisters in Christ. Having such a heart of compassion means that we will allow the Holy Spirit to use us as instruments of hope and healing when our spiritual siblings are struggling and their joy seems elusive.

Do you know how stereotypes are developed? They are constructed as people recognize certain repeated and predictable patterns of behavior. Some professional sports teams, regardless of the fact that they have new players each year, have a stereotypical reputation as bullies, or cheaters, or poor sports. The repeated predictable pattern of *some* of the players has established an uncomplimentary reputation for the entire team.

For Christians, one of the unpleasant and unbiblical stereotypes that the unsaved world has assigned to us is this *Christians are the only people who shoot their wounded.* Ouch! That's a terrible thing to be known for, but the stereotype didn't just originate out of nowhere. It came from the observation of outsiders who watched Christians allow their brothers and sisters to struggle and fail, without stepping in to offer help and hope.

It isn't just unbelievers who identify that unpleasant stereotype about Christians. There are those sitting in our churches who dread every service. Instead of feeling safe and cared for by the body, these precious believers live in fear and distrust of the members. Counselor Ed Welch says this:

Have you ever noticed that for many people, church as family doesn't exist? More often I overhear people who talk as if the church were their enemy. Sometimes these people have been hurt by people in the church and then make a decision not to be hurt again. They generalize from the specific case to the entire church: If one person hurt me, then the church hurt me.

We must change that stereotype. We must examine the hurtful ways that we approach one another's circumstances and replace those methods with Biblical sympathy and grace. Consider for a moment some of our hurtful responses to difficult circumstances. At times, we try to fit another believer's trial into the template of our own experiences. When we do so, we run the risk of offering faulty counsel that isn't helpful for their particular situation. *After all, it worked for us … Shouldn't it work for them?* Sometimes, we question our brethren to see if sin has brought about their situation. Really?? The Holy Spirit can bring conviction if that's the case … He doesn't need any Junior-Holy-Spirits-in-Training. A wise Biblical counselor can ask the right questions to determine an individual's own personal culpability for their circumstances. Our friends just don't need that type of judgment from us. What they need is help, hope, and loving encouragement to see their circumstances through the lens of the Scriptures.

The more prepared we are to personally do battle with the enemy of our own joy, the more prepared we will be to help others do the same. We will learn to recognize our own red flags of danger. But just as importantly, we'll recognize the danger signs of others who are unable to realize the joy that is rightfully theirs. Then, when one of the members of the body is struggling to find joy in the midst of a difficult circumstance, we won't be like Job's friends, adding to their sorrow. Once we've received the gentle ministry of the Holy Spirit for ourselves, we will long to minister that same hope to others. Instead of becoming tools for Satan, we can become the physical hands and feet of Jesus.

What hurting believers need is our fellowship. They need us to lead them gently to the promises of God. Sometimes, they just need us to sit beside them, listen, and then escort them to the throne of grace through prayer. We can exhort them to take their gaze off their situation, but we certainly shouldn't tell them to *Just Get Over It!* Remember, even when their unhappiness seems small or trivial, to them it is huge and overwhelming. If it's a big deal to them, it must become a big deal to us if we are to minister to them wisely.

We have the tremendous privilege of pointing our hurting friends to the truth about God. We can all remember a time that God seemed distant, and His promises seemed ineffectual in our own personal lives. Remembering those times will help us to walk alongside our fellow strugglers with compassion and Biblical sympathy. Jeremy Pierre explains it this way:

"Whether people realize it or not, their story is not primarily

about them, but about the God who made them. People were created with the supreme purpose of loving God with the full extent of their dynamic functions; so, every use of those dynamic functions can be measured by how it conforms to this supreme purpose. But the sad presence of sin makes people's hearts inclined away from God. They do not naturally perceive God rightly."

Our greatest purpose as we minister to our friends is to help them perceive God rightly. When they are able to do so, they will be able to develop an eternal perspective about their trials and circumstances. We're never called to be judge and jury of their situation. Instead, we have the opportunity to walk into their circumstance gently and circumspectly. We have the honor to remind them of their God and of His promises of good toward them. In their time of need, we can represent Christ by bringing His Word and His joy to shine light into the darkness of their circumstances.

When we begin to do that, slowly but surely the world's stereotype of the church's propensity to shoot our wounded will begin to change. Instead of seeing us as uncaring and self-centered, the world will finally see the church as God intended, ministers of grace, peace, and joy to one another out of obedience to Christ.

Personal Application:

- Begin your own list of God's promises of everlasting relationship with you. Make cards and place them strategically around you home so that when you need them, you have them at your fingertips!

- Do you have other women who fit the *true*

fellowship mold? Such a friend is truly a treasure! Find a pretty card and send them a snail mail message of thankfulness for their friendship. Be specific as you share the spiritual help and hope they provide for you.

• It's that time, again! Add another memory verse to your growing list.

13

WELCOME TO JOYFUL STREET

> *od promises specifically to be with us in our sorrows*
> *and afflictions. He will not spare us from the waters*
> *of sorrow and the fires of adversity, but He will go*
> *through them with us.*

– *Jerry Bridges*

I TRUST by now that we're all on the same page. We've *got it*–
joy is our permanent possession because of our relationship
with Christ. We understand that there are certain acts of
obedience that will cause our joy to grow and flourish.
We've resting in the knowledge that although trials and
unhappiness are a certainty in this life, none of them will
ever be able to defeat our Captain Jesus. We're learning to
recognize the red flags of danger, and we're putting into
practice the actions that will best protect our joy.

But sometimes ... Sometimes we just need to know
where to find our joy! Psalm 16:11 pronounces an unques-

tionable truth: *In Your presence is fullness of joy.* The Bible says it, so I believe it. But sometimes, I just want to *see it.* Even though I believe it, I need to know what it means to find joy in the presence of Jesus on Tuesday afternoon when I'm tired, and over-scheduled, and my day is headed in a bad direction. Where is the presence of Jesus, then?

Do you have somewhere that always causes your heart to beat happily? Is there a certain place that fills your happy-tank? When I was a little girl, my Uncle Bob and Aunt Marge's home provided that type of happiness for my heart. I grew up in an untidy, unhygienic, super cluttered house. My mom seriously believed that everyone had it out for us, so our drapes were always closed and the house always dark. It wasn't a particularly pleasant place for a little girl with an over-active imagination.

But my uncle and aunt's house was so different. It was clean, and bright, and smelled good. Things were organized, the food was yummy, and both my aunt and uncle loved inviting others into their home. Every summer for two weeks, I would go visit in that wonderful, safe sanctuary of peace. As soon as I arrived, it was as though the stress of my own home just fell off of my shoulders.

When I became an adult, our family's yearly rental house in Bethany Beach offered that same type of feeling. Although I looked forward to the salty air and loved the sound of the waves, there was something else about that house that took me back to my childhood and my happy days with my uncle and aunt. For years, I just couldn't put my finger on what it was ...

Then I figured it out! My uncle and aunt's house had a stone driveway. Whenever I heard the crunch of those white stones under the tires of my uncle's car, I knew that I was HOME. Regardless of the fact that my visits were only for two weeks, for that small amount of time, I felt more at home and secure than I ever felt in my parent's house. *Our beach rental had the same stone driveway.* That was why I immediately felt at home! As our 15-passenger van pulled on to the white stone driveway, the crunching stones awakened my memories of my uncle and aunt's home and filled my heart with peace and happiness.

The happiness I found in both of those homes was certainly a circumstantial happiness. It was happiness, not joy that filled my heart. But in the same manner, we all need a place where we can pull into the driveway and hear the sound of joy under our tires. God has graciously provided the addresses for several such locations in His Word. Let's follow His directions and visit some joyful destinations.

This last chapter truly is a roadmap of sorts. The Scriptures do provide us some residences, or destinations if you will, that are places that we can consistently rediscover our joy. It isn't that our joy is new at these locations, but sometimes, we just need to be reminded of some forgotten sites of Biblical joy. When we know where to look, we'll be successful in the search to discover (or rediscover) our joy. It's there waiting, so let's unfold our map and get going.

I haven't put these destinations in any particular order, but this first destination is, for me, the most precious of them all. Earlier this afternoon, I took a break from writing and hopped on to my Facebook account. I had a notification waiting for me. Today, a precious friend and Godly minister of the gospel went home to the Lord after a struggle with cancer. Even writing those words makes my heart hurt. I glanced through the many, many comments that had been sent to his wife. Comment after comment, although grieving his loss, pointed to the joy that was now his because of his salvation. One after another, his Christian friends were repeating this truth: *We do not mourn as those who have no hope!* (I Thessalonians 4:13)

The hope of our salvation is the permanent residence of joy. May we never lose the awe of that truth! When one of my daughters was young, each time she was called upon to pray, she began by thanking the Lord for her salvation. That's who I want to be. I want to be a girl who never loses her awe over her salvation. Our salvation is the security for our future and a storehouse of joy.

The Scriptures are rich with reminders of the joy that is secured by our salvation. I Peter 1:8–9 is one such passage:

AND THOUGH YOU *have not seen Him, you love Him, and though you do not see Him now, but believe in Him, you greatly rejoice with joy inexpressible and full of glory, obtaining s the outcome of your faith the salvation of your souls.*

Do you see the adjective that is used to describe our joy in this passage? Our joy will be inexpressible. We can't even picture the joy that is to be ours as a result of our salvation. This earthly joy is just a dim picture of the joy that will fill our hearts when we finally see our Savior face to face.

Remember, Luke 15:10 taught us that the *angels rejoice over the salvation of even one soul.* What unselfish joy! The angels can never experience salvation, and they can never be known as the Sons of God. However, their understanding of the greatness of Christ's sacrifice on our behalf causes them to be filled with joy.

Psalm 70:4 teaches that the *continual outpouring of rejoicing over our salvation* will cause God to be magnified. As we experience joy, God is made *bigger* to a watching and

unsaved world. The Bible study at the end of the book will
give an even more in-depth look at what the Scriptures have
to say about our joy and its permanent abode within salvation. For now, though, may we become women who spend
time daily lingering in the joy of our salvation.

The next destination of joy may be a bit of a surprise. I
don't normally think of the same-old/same-old activities of
my daily life as particularly joyful, but the Word of God
teaches us otherwise. The New International Version translates Ecclesiastes 9:7 like this:

*Go, eat your food with gladness, and drink your wine with a
joyful heart, for God has already approved what you do.*

WHEN WE ARE WALKING FAITHFULLY with the Lord
throughout our days, we can trust that our daily activities
are within His approval. According to Ecclesiastes, that
approval will provide us with a joyful heart. Our families
need wives and moms with joyful hearts. Whether circumstances are hiding our joy, or whether we are simply
squashing our joy because of doubt or fear, our daily activities must become a dwelling place for joy.

Sometimes, when I'm struggling to hold on to my joy or
when it's just plain hidden from sight, the best thing I can
do is get up off the couch and get busy. Engaging our minds
and hands in useful service to our families can bring us joy
and help us to get our minds off our circumstances. No, you
can't *work* your trials away, but we sure can *work out our
salvation with fear and trembling.* (Philippians 2:12) And as we
now know, where there is salvation ... There Is Joy!

The other reason that joy resides in daily life is simply because each day is a *day that the Lord has made.* (Psalm 118:24) Each day is God's precious possession, and we can rejoice and be glad because He has chosen to include us in His day. After living in Northern New England with the long, gray winters, I struggle mightily when the clouds roll in and the sun is hidden from view. Psalm 118 reminds me that *each and every day*, whether sunny, gloomy, or in between, belongs to the Lord. That truth alone is a safe haven to which I can run for shelter and find my joy.

God intends our relationships with other believers to be a safe place where we can find joy to help us in time of need. However, not only are we to find joy in relationship with them, they are to be refreshed and filled with joy after spending time with us. Seriously, it's a win-win situation. In II John 1:12, John was able to be confident that when he arrived to visit with the *chosen lady and her children,* they would find joy in his presence. I think that confidence came from his commitment to bringing joy to his fellow believers. Even Paul, who so often had to deliver hard messages, was confident that his relationship with other Christians was joy-producing.

The only way that we can have that same confidence is by carefully stewarding our Christian friendships. Even the closest friendships don't afford us the freedom to *let down our hair* and loosen our Biblical standards. If we are to be a sanctuary of joy to others, we must be motivated by love and constrained by the Holy Spirit.

Quite frankly, when my joy-tank is running low, reading biographies of Christians who walked before me can become a joy-destination for my heart. When we read of their sacrifices of service and of the Lord's blessing upon their obedience, our hearts will be encouraged and filled with joy. The Apostle Paul experienced this type of joy when he received an account of Philemon's ministry to the brethren. (Philemon 1:7) Philemon's obedience produced a *haven of joy* for the tired apostle.

Along those same lines, the younger believers to whom we minister will soon become *our joy*. Paul wrote this to the young believers in the Thessalonian church:

> *For who is our hope or joy or crown of exultation? Is it not even you, in the presence of our Lord Jesus at His coming? For you are our glory and joy.*
> —*I Thessalonians 2:19–20*

THIS IS the picture of a double-blessing. As Paul ministered to the Thessalonians, they found joy in their relationship with him and in the truths that he shared with them. For Paul, the growth and obedience of the Thessalonian believers filled his heart with joy and exultation. That type of Christian relationship truly brings glory to God and shows Christ to the world.

Simple Christian fellowship definitely provides joy. However, perhaps even more joy and blessing are found in the discipling relationships between older and younger believers. Knowing that those to whom we are offering truth are growing in their relationship and obedience to the Lord will give our hearts an injection of joy. Let's examine the words of the Lord Jesus in John 15:8–11:

> *By this is my Father glorified, that you bear much fruit, and so*

prove to be My disciples. Just as the Father has loved Me, I have
also loved you; abide in My love. If you keep My commandments,
you will abide in My love; just as I have kept My Father's
commandments, and abide in His love. These things I have
spoken to you, and that your joy may be made full.

THERE TRULY IS NO GREATER joy than watching younger believers grow in their relationship with the Lord. During this time of self-quarantining during the Covid-19 pandemic, there are a few things that I'm just really missing. Right at the top of the list is the time I spend each week with several young women. Digging into the Scriptures with them and watching them allow the Lord to mold and change them, brings me such joy. I truly understand what the Apostles Paul and John felt when they addressed younger believers as *My Children*.

Anyone who has heard me speak knows that the passion of my heart is discipleship. If you truly want to be filled with joy, begin to pour truth into the life of a younger believer! Discipleship is a conduit for the fullness of joy to cascade into the life of both the one leading the discipleship and the disciple. Actually, the expanded outline of this book was developed as I walked a new mom through the hard trial of postpartum depression. Learning about the obedience of joy was an avenue for hope and healing from her darkness.

I want to conclude this chapter with one final and permanent joy-destination and residence. In the same way in which the beauty of joy is firmly enthroned in our salvation, it is just as beautifully situated in our future hope in Christ. Because of Christ's righteousness imputed to us, we can have the expectation of joy and gladness. Considering our home-to-be in heaven with Jesus should excite us and make us long to go to be with Him. Salvation and Heaven are the bookends of our joy.

Today, as I mourn the death of my friend, I have to admit that a small part of my heart envies him. No more pain, no more suffering, no more trials or hardships ... He's made it to the goal, and now he sees his Lord face-to-face. As the Apostle Paul affirmed for all of us who long for the Lord's coming, *I prefer to be present with the Lord and absent from the body*. (II Corinthians 5:8)

The more we understand and take ownership of our joy–the gift of God to every believer, the more we will long to be with the Giver of the gift! Jesus is our joy. What an unspeakable joy will be ours when we see Him face to face!

Don't despair on those days when joy seems to be lacking. Remember that God has placed our joy in permanent dwelling places. They aren't hard to find, and they aren't hidden from our view. All we have to do is return to those familiar stomping grounds. Joy waits for us each and every day in our salvation. It meets us in our obedient daily activities. Joy is available because each day is a gift from God's gracious hand. Joy shines in our Biblical relationships with other believers. And finally, we can entrust our joy to the hope of our future home with Christ. Truly, God has prepared sanctuaries of joy to bless and encourage us during this journey through life!

PERSONAL APPLICATION:

- Do you long for your future home in heaven? Sometimes, we don't long for it because we simply don't know what to expect when we get there. Your only big assignment this week is to look up verses about heaven and record what you learn in the space provided. Have fun discovering the joy that is to come!

- I said only *big assignment* ... You still have to add a memory verse to your list!

AFTERWORD

It's Time to Land this Baby

What a journey. Oh, how I pray that this study has been a blessing to your heart. I hope that you'll use this book and your notes and homework over and over in the years to come. On those days when joy seems elusive, please allow these truths to help you regain your focus and snatch joy back into your white-knuckled grasp.

Joy is so contagious! Now that you've completed this study, I encourage you to go through it again soon with a friend, co-worker, or family member. Teaching someone else what you've learned will cement the Biblical truths in your heart and mind. As you share the joy you've discovered through your interaction with the Word of God, that joy will become a sweet gift to those whom you love.

We live in a sometimes harsh and always fallen world. At times, that hard, sin-stained world will again tempt you to think that joy has slipped through your fingertips. Remember, because of God's salvation provided through Christ's atoning death and based on the faithful promises of God ...

Joy Is Yours! You own it, and no one can ever take it away from you. As God's gift to you, it is always available and freely given for your benefit.

Never let go of your joy; battle on because joy is worth the fight!

Fixing our eyes on Jesus, the author and perfecter of faith, who for the joy set before Him endured the cross, despising the shame, and has sat down at the right hand of the throne of God. —
Hebrews 12:12

STUDY QUESTIONS

CHAPTER ONE STUDY QUESTIONS

- In one or two sentences, define what joy means to you. Don't simply copy the definition from the book! I want you to carefully consider how you identify joy and how that definition affects your actions and emotions daily.

- Read Deuteronomy 33:28. This verse tells us what God provides, how He cares for us in that provision, and whom He protects us from while He is caring for us. Record those three insights in the space below.

- Read Romans 8:37–39. These verses are a reminder of the dangers that believers face daily. However, the verses also state clearly the

outcome of the battle. In the space below, record
both the risks and the result.

- The truth of John 3:16 is the foundation of our
  eternal security and promise of joy. In the space
  provided, share your testimony of salvation in 5–
  10 sentences.

- Sometimes, it's hard to self-evaluate to determine whether or not we are exhibiting joy through our attitudes and actions. That's where the observation of a spouse, trusted friend, or even our children can be of invaluable help. Ask someone whom you trust whether or not they would describe you as a joyful and joy-filled person. Especially for those of us who tend to be quieter or somewhat melancholy, what we think we're showing others and what shows forth through our actions are two different things!

- From the text of the book, write out the definition of joy. What two elements work together to produce joy in our lives? Is it possible to have a joyful attitude without joyful actions accompanying that attitude? Or, is it possible to have joyful reactions without a joyful heart? Record your thoughts below.

- This last question is personal. Make a list of those activities that produce joy in your life. After making your list, consider how you would react if those actions or activities disappeared. Please, be honest with yourself! Ask God to show you whether or not you have an unhealthy attachment to happiness. Next, make a list of those things in your life that produce joy. Behind these "joy-producers" record the Scripture that shows they are based on your settled relationship of salvation and upon the eternal promises of God.

CHAPTER TWO STUDY QUESTIONS

- Read Ephesians 1:1–23; Philippians 1:1–11; and Colossians 1:1–9. Record your observations of these chapters, including especially those words of affirmation that the Apostle Paul shared with his readers.

- Now, read Galatians 1:1–12; Galatians 3:1–5, and 4:11–20. In the space provided, record your observations of these sections of Scripture. How did Paul write to the Galatian believers; what was his tone? What actions of the Galatian church did Paul condemn?

- I don't know about you, but I wouldn't want to receive a letter like the letter that the Galatian church received! Consider the areas of condemnation in that church? Are any of the actions that caused Paul to rebuke those believers present in your own life? If so, may I encourage you to stop now and confess those areas to the Lord? Don't press on without stopping to seek forgiveness and restoring your relationship with God. If it is helpful, use the space provided to write out your prayer of repentance.

- Read Matthew 5:13–16. According to these verses, believers are to be the representation of God's light in the world. When we are joyfully exhibiting that light, we bring glory to God. What do you think is the result when our joy is diminished or even blocked out? Use the space below to record any things that you have allowed to block out your Christ-honoring light. After listing your insights, consider what practical steps you can take to eliminate those things from your life.

- The responses that God expects from His children are often counter-intuitive. They go against our nature. Left to our own devices, we would never choose to respond Biblically. What are some counter-intuitive choices that God is asking you to make right now? It's so helpful to have Scripture to help us make those choices that seem so opposite to our nature. Record two or three choices that God has placed before you and use your concordance to find the Biblical reason or precedent behind that choice.

- Counter-intuitive choices will often open wide the door for us to testify of God's work in our lives. When friends or family members ask us WHY we make the choices that we make, we have the opportunity to share with them about our trustworthy God who helps us to live in a manner that is different than the rest of the world. It's so easy to take credit for ourselves, but when we use our counter-intuitive choices to point to God, the Lord receives all of the glory. Record an opportunity you had to share about God because of a decision or choice you made that was contrary to the norm.

CHAPTER THREE STUDY QUESTIONS

- Consider the quote at the top of the chapter. Are you actively pursuing joy? Sometimes, it's helpful to see on paper those actions we are taking to ensure that joy is part of our lives. Record those actions below.

- Read I Thessalonians 5:16. Record the verse below.

- Now, read Romans 5:3; Luke 10:20; Acts 16:33–34; and Luke 15:10. What are things listed in these verses that are the cause of rejoicing? Record them below.

- Read Isaiah 61:10; Luke 1:46–49; and Psalm 145:1–7. Who is worthy to receive our rejoicing? According to these verses, list some of God's attributes that make Him worthy of praise and rejoicing.

- Sometimes, it's just plain hard to rejoice. However, we are enabled to rejoice because of a specific gift that was given to us by the Lord. Read Acts 10:46. When the believers received the Holy Spirit, how did they speak of their God?

- Read I Corinthians 10:31. In the space provided, make a list of six specific ways that you can bring glory to God through your daily activities. God receives the glory, and we are personally blessed when we turn the mundane tasks of life into channels of celebration to God.

- Bible reading, prayer, Scripture memorization, and service to others are all ways that we can build our spiritual muscle memory. Considering these four listed ways of bulking up, is there one area that needs some more focused attention? If so, write below your action plan for working out that particular spiritual muscle.

- Evaluate this statement: Everything, whether good or bad, that comes into your life has already passed through the approval process of God? Is there any situation that you are facing that seems beyond His approval? It's reassuring to know that He's not surprised by, and He doesn't already know the good that each hard circumstance will bring into our lives. In the space below, may I encourage you to write a prayer committing to bring God glory while at the same time trusting Him to bring about good from your situation?

CHAPTER FOUR STUDY QUESTIONS

- Read Romans 12:2. Transformation by God, rather than conformation to the world, we will show forth God's will. What does this verse say about the will of God?
- Can you think of a time that you were able to bring joy into another person(s) difficult situation? In a few sentences, describe how joy changed the course of that hard circumstance.

- Joy always begins from the inside out. What are some ways that people try to change outwardly without being transformed inwardly? Record those ways, then make a note of any dangers that come from such an outward-only transformation.
- Read both Isaiah 48:20 and Jeremiah 51:6. In these verses, the prophets share two critical reasons that the people were to return to the land. Record those reasons below.

Refusing to return to the Lord sets us up for two hard consequences. First, we are unable to testify about God's protection and provision. Secondly, when we remain in places or attitudes that are dishonoring to God, we run the risk of reaping the consequences of that decision.

- Read Proverbs 5:22–23 and record what you learn from these verses.

When sin binds us, it's crucial to recognize that our imprisonment doesn't come from outside of ourselves. According to this verse, we are entangled by the sin that belongs to us.

- This question is personal, so don't feel any pressure to share your answer with anyone else. (Unless you're comfortable doing so and you think it would be of benefit to someone else, which I'm pretty sure it would be ☺) Have you ever experience God's chastening because you refused to return to Him and His will? Share in a few sentences the result of your choice.

- Read Ecclesiastes 4:9–10. There is no such thing as a Lone Ranger Christian; we need the encouragement and accountability that comes from strong Christian friendships. When we are falling into disobedience by refusing to return to the Lord, a dedicated sister-in-Christ can give us the kick-in-the-pants that we need to make the right decision. Do you have that type of friend? Take this opportunity to write them a handwritten note of thanks for their friendship.

CHAPTER FIVE STUDY QUESTIONS

1. Read Luke 2:10–11. Restate this verse in your own words in the space provided. If you were bringing such glorious news to the shepherds have would you have phrased your message of joy?

W hat a relief it is to know that we don't have to produce our joy. Joy was formed and brought to earth as the precious gift of the Father.

1. God's desire is for His children to experience joy each day. In the space below, list three practical actions that you can take today to experience the joy that the Holy Spirit provides.

- Prayer, obedience, and joy are intrinsically linked together. Read Proverbs 15:8–9. Record below what you learn from these verses. How does God feel about our prayers? Practically speaking, what does it look like to pursue righteousness? Can we seek righteousness apart from obedience?

- Read James 4:17. The opposite of obedience is disobedience, and this verse unapologetically names disobedience as sin. In your own experience, what is the result of willful disregard of God's commands? Can joy coexist with disobedience?

- Unlike joy, happiness can coexist with disobedience. Throughout the book of Proverbs, the fool delights in his rebellion and willful choices. Read Proverbs 10:23; 17:28; 14:16; and 15:21. In the space provided, make a list of the things that you learn about the life of the fool.

Now that you've completed your list of the fool's characteristics, spend some reflective time in prayer. Ask the Lord to expose any areas of foolishness in your life that are a result of self-will. In particular, seek God's wisdom to discern those foolish choices that are squashing your Christ-given joy.

- Read Galatians 5:13. List any exceptions to serving provided for us in this verse. Is there anyone excluded from the list of those whom we should help? This question is for-your-eyes-only: Is there someone you refuse to serve. How, out of love for your Lord, can you begin to serve that person. Record a practical action-step for service below.

- Read Ephesians 4:22–24 and record the two actions that each believer must perform in their life. One of the most helpful tools for growth is a permanent "Put-off/Put-on" list. I have mine in a notebook tucked into the front of my Bible. Each time the Lord shows me an area that I need to abandon, I put that area on my put-off list. Then, I search the Scriptures to find the appropriate put-on Biblical trait to replace what I've discontinued. May I encourage you to start your notebook today?

- Read Philippians 3:16 and write out the verse in the space provided. Is there any area of conviction in your life that has become "less convicting" as time goes on? Although there may be actions that change over time, we must be sure that the change came about because of God's leading, not merely because we are "forgetful" of what God called us to in the first place. This verse is a great memory verse that the Holy Spirit can use to bring to remembrance what we learned previously.

CHAPTER SIX STUDY QUESTIONS

1. Consider this quote from Elizabeth Elliott: "God will never disappoint us. He loves us and has only one purpose for us: holiness, which in His kingdom equals joy." Reword those sentences in a way that is meaningful to you. Do we consider holiness to be joyful? Under your reworded statement, make a list of what our culture deems necessary for joy.

- Make a list of five "non-negotiable" convictions in your life. Then, find the Biblical basis for those convictions. It's vitally important to base our convictions on the Word of God, not on what others do or how we just assume that we must live.

- Read Psalm 119:11 and record what you learn from this verse. Why is it so important to memorize Scripture? From what does the Word, hidden in our hearts, protect us? What is the last verse that you memorized? Write it out in the space below.

- Read James 1:22–24. In your own words, explain how obeying the Word of God acts as a mirror to our hearts.

- Do you know any women who "abound" with joy? What does that "abounding" look like in real life? If possible, find some time to engage these women in conversation. Ask them what it is that makes it possible for them to overflow with joy. Record their answers and see if there is a common thread in their lives that would increase the joy in your own life.

- Read John 15:4–11 and make a list of all of the blessings that are ours when we abide with Christ.

CHAPTER SEVEN STUDY QUESTIONS

- Read Luke 6:45 and record the contrast shown in
  this verse. What comes out of our mouths is an
  accurate indication of what is going on inside of
  our hearts. Our words and actions show others
  clearly whether or not we are putting Biblical
  truth into action.
- Read Galatians 6:9 and write out the verse in the
  space below. Is there any "doing good" that is
  proving to be overwhelmingly wearying? Record
  it below, then write out a prayer handing that
  problematic situation over to the Lord. One of
  God's greatest desires is that we would reap joy
  from our circumstances, and He is eager to help
  us along the way!

- Surrendering has many different applications. Read the following verses and record both what Believers must surrender and God's blessing in response to that surrender.

- James 4:10
- I Peter 5:6
- Romans 12:1
- I Corinthians 6:19–20
- Luke 9:23–24
- Proverbs 3:5–6

- Just as prayer, obedience, and joy link together, so too, trust, obedience, and joy are joined. Read Romans 12:9–14 and make a list of the actions found within those verses.

I f we don't trust God's kind heart on our behalf, none of those actions make any sense. In the eyes of the world, we are nothing more than do-gooders at best and doormats at worst. However, because the love of God compels us, we can be poured out for others, and that very emptying will allow us to rejoice in God. What a wonderful gift it is to serve and trust the Lord!

1. Write out the definition of hope, as found in the text of the book. Below, construct a list of those things that you are hoping for and waiting for God to provide.

CHAPTER EIGHT STUDY QUESTIONS

- Seeking wisdom is the pathway to joy. However, if we can't recognize the difference between wisdom and foolishness, we risk walking down the wrong path. Read James 3:17 and record the descriptions of wisdom according to this verse.

- From the list above, choose one specific attribute of wisdom and use your concordance to find three verses that speak to that form of wisdom. Write out the references to those three verses below.

- The more we know about God, the more we will truly worship Him. Google the attributes of God. Choose three attributes and find at least two verses that speak to each of them. Record what you discover in the space below.

1. What acts of service do you perform regularly? Consider those acts of service and answer the following questions:

- Are the acts of service I perform behind the scenes or upfront?

- Whom do I serve?

- Do I serve out of love for Christ, or am I fulfilling needs because "someone has to do it ..."?

- Are there other areas of service that I could perform?

After answering the above questions, spend some time in prayer. Ask the Lord to show you whether or not you are serving Him humbly and with a thankful heart. Is all of your service in front of an audience? If so, consider adding some service that is behind the scenes, and vice versa.

CHAPTER NINE STUDY QUESTIONS

- I hope this first question is enjoyable to answer! Have you ever "made a memorial" to recognize the growth that God has brought about in your life? If not, I'd encourage you to stop right now and do so. Perhaps you will write a prayer of thanksgiving, or make a card to keep in your Bible, or go and tell a friend what God has done in your life. Regardless of how you choose to memorialize your growth, doing so will make that growth a permanent memory to spur you on to even more good deeds.

- Read John 8:31 and record what you learn from the verse. In your own words, explain what it means to "continue" in Christ's Word.

- Colossians 2:6 outlines another way that we can abide with Christ. What is this way?

- Read I John 2:28. What is the contrast shown in this verse? According to the verse, why is it essential to make sure that we are always in a position of abiding?

- The opposite of abiding is fretting. What are the personal physical manifestations that show that you are worrying, rather than abiding? Do you recognize when fretting is taking control of your life?

- Philippians 4:6 is the perfect antidote to worrying and fretting. Write out the verse below. What attitude must accompany our prayers and petitions? Why do you think this attitude is so important?

- In what ways has the Lord gifted you to work for Him? Have you carefully considered how best to work for God? List your areas of giftedness below, then beside each entry record, how you are using that specific gift for the Lord. If you're

uncertain of your gifts and talents, ask a trusted
friend or your spouse for their helpful input.

- One final question for consideration ... Is there
anything in your life that is keeping you from
freely working for the Lord? If so, how can you
disentangle yourself from something that may be
good, in order to focus on that which is best
wholeheartedly?

CHAPTER TEN STUDY QUESTIONS

- This question is just a (sort of) fun question. How do you picture joy? Take a few moments and write a paragraph defining what joy "looks like" for you.

- Unhappiness clouds our Joy-vision. Scripture is the light that cuts through that discouraging cloud. In the space provided, write out Jeremiah 29:11.

- Consider the verse above: what circumstances are threatening to obscure your joy from view? Write out any such things and use your concordance to find the Biblical solution to your joy-clouding situation.

- This question may seem a bit strange but bear with me for a moment. Sometimes, our difficult circumstances cause us to miss the hard things that threaten our family and friends. Spend a few moments listing hard situations that you know are being dealt with by your loved ones. After making your list, stop, and pray for your hurting family and friends.

- This chapter is full of "to-do" activities! From your list above, pick four people and write them a note of encouragement. Let them know that you are praying for them and precisely what you prayed. Assure them of your continued prayer on their behalf!

- In this chapter, we studied various individuals who faced hardships and trials. Choose another character in the Scriptures and record both the hard circumstance that they faced, as well as God's solution to that situation.

- At the end of the chapter, you were encouraged to spend some time praising the Lord. Psalm 22:3

states that God inhabits the praise of His people. Isn't that a beautiful picture? In the space below, record some of the things truths about God that caused you to praise Him.

CHAPTER ELEVEN STUDY QUESTIONS

- Proverbs 22:3 provides a warning to the wise. Write out the verse below. After recording the verse, may I encourage you to consider your own life? Often, we blame our hard circumstances on other people or misfortune. However, many times, we face hardships because we continue to wander over and over into the same sinful traps. Only you and the Lord can determine whether or not that "naïve" person is you ... Spend time seeking God's wisdom to self-evaluate carefully.

- Although Satan longs to see God's children fail, we do not need to fear him. Read Revelation 12:9 and record what you learn from this verse.

- Read James 4:7. What is the outcome when we are submitted to God and resisting the devil?

- Read Revelation 12:10. Is there anything in your life that is an avenue for Satan's accusations? If so, record them below, and after each allegation, write out I John 1:9. There is nothing in the life of the believer that is beyond the forgiveness of God!

- Busyness will distract and exhaust us. Busyness robs us of joy and peace. Read John 14:27 and record what you learn from the verse.

- Busyness and a lack of margins in our lives can become so "normal" that we don't even notice how much we're running, Running, RUNNING! To finish out this chapter, spend some time listing EVERYTHING that demands your time and attention during the week. (Be Honest!) Include time spent at work, on social media, serving, etc. After making your list, ask your husband or a trusted friend to look over your weekly activities to help you to assess whether or not you're just too busy.

CHAPTER TWELVE STUDY QUESTIONS

- Read Hebrews 11:1 and record what you learn
  from this verse. Does it seem counter-intuitive to
  place your faith in something that you
  cannot see?

- Considering the above verse: In your own words,
  describe any pitfalls you think would accompany
  a faith that must be seen to be believed.

- What verse most clearly reassures you of God's
  love for you? Record that verse in the space
  below.

- Just as my husband was able to reassure Molly's

heart by his affirming words of love toward her, so too, we can be instruments of reassurance to others. Find some verses that speak of God's love and write them out on cards. After you've written the cards, pray and ask the Lord, who could use the reassurance of His love for them. After praying, remember to take the final step and mail the cards!

- Read Matthew 11:28–30. According to these verses, the Lord longs to give us rest. However, what acts of our obedience precede His gift of rest?

- An eternal perspective will refocus us when we temptation to despair looms menacingly. Read John 14:3. This verse states four things that should give us hope for our eternity. Record these four truths in the space below.

CHAPTER THIRTEEN STUDY QUESTIONS

1. Knowing where we can go to find the Lord is a safeguard for our troubled hearts. Consider the verses below and record all of the dwelling places of our God.

- Psalm 11:4–7

- Exodus 15:17

- Psalm 26:8

- Psalm 84 (One of my favorite Psalms!)

- I Chronicles 23:25

- Regardless of where God is dwelling, He is our permanent and continual source of joy! Let's finish out this study by composing a prayer of gratitude for all the God has provided, and by committing to fiercely and steadfastly snatch and hold on to our joy!

QUOTABLE QUOTES

(And some really great books that should land on your bookshelves!)

Introduction

Piper, John. Desiring God. Oregon: Multnomah, 2003, p. 54.

Chapter One

Berg, Jim. Changed Into His Image: God's Plan For Transforming Your Life, 2nd edition. Greenville: JourneyForth, 2018, p. 113.

Tozer, A. W. The Knowledge of the Holy. New York: Harper Collins, 1961, p. 102.

Chapter Two

Packer, J. I. Knowing God. Downers Grove: IVP Books, 1973, p. 25.

Chapter Three

Piper, John. Desiring God. Oregon: Multnomah, 2003, p. 26.

Chapter Four

Berg, Jim. Changed Into His Image: God's Plan For Transforming Your Life, 2nd edition. Greenville: JourneyForth, 2018, p. 112.

Pierre, Jeremy. The Dynamic Heart in Daily Life: Connecting Christ to Human Experience. Greensboro: New Growth Press, 2016, p. 147.

Piper, John. Desiring God. Oregon: Multnomah, 2003, p. 22.

Chapter Five

Jensen, Margaret. First We Have Coffee: And Then We Talk. Eugene: Harvest House, 1995, p. 44.

Chapter Six

Bridges, Jerry. The Discipline of Grace: God's Role and Our Role in the Pursuit of Holiness. Colorado Springs: NavPress, 2006, p. 118–119.

Weirsbe, Warren W. Be Joyful: Evan When Things Go Wrong You Can Have Joy. Wheaton: Victor Books, 1984, p. 73.

Chapter Seven

Bridges, Jerry. Trusting God: Even When Life Hurts. Colorado Springs: NavPress, 2008, p. 16.

Keller, Timothy. Anchored in Christ. Online search.

McDowell, Josh and Dale Bellis. Evidence for Joy: Unlocking the Secrets of Being Loved, Accepted and Secure. Waco: Word, 1984, p. 154.

Murray, Andrew. Absolute Surrender: How to Walk in Perfect Peace. New Kensington: Whittaker House, 1981, p. 7.

Chapter Eight

Elliot, Elizabeth. Discipline: The Glad Surrender. Grand Rapids: Revell, 1999, p. 122, 155.

Chapter Nine

Elliot, Elizabeth. Discipline: The Glad Surrender. Grand Rapids: Revell, 1999, p. 125.

Murray, Andrew. Absolute Surrender: How to Walk in Perfect Peace. New Kensington: Whittaker House, 1981, p. 10, 76.

Chapter Ten

Tozer, A. W. The Knowledge of the Holy. New York: Harper-Collins, 1961, p. 81.

Chapter Eleven

Bridges, Jerry. Trusting God: Even When Life Hurts. Colorado Springs: NavPress, 2008, p. 202.

Welch, Edward T. When People are Big and God is Small: Overcoming Peer Pressure, Codependency, and the Fear of Man. Philippsburg: P and R Publishing, 1997, p. 183.

Chapter Twelve

Murray, Andrew. Absolute Surrender: How to Walk in Perfect Peace. New Kensington: Whittaker House, 1981, p. 121.

Pierre, Jeremy. The Dynamic Heart in Daily Life: Connecting Christ to Human Experience. Greensboro: New Growth Press, 2016, p. 73, 189.

Chapter Thirteen

Bridges, Jerry. Trusting God: Even When Life Hurts. Colorado Springs: NavPress, 2008, p. 47.

ABOUT THE AUTHOR

Megan Ann Scheibner is an experienced author of counseling and faith based non-fiction books. You can reach Megan directly at MeganScheibner.com.

Biography of Megan Scheibner

Megan was born March 13th 1962 and came home to her adoptive family March 15th. She grew up in York, PA and graduated from York Suburban H.S. in 1980. Four years later, she earned a B.A. in Speech Communications from West Chester University. After homeschooling her eight children for 24+ years, Megan returned to school and received a Masters in Biblical Counseling. She is currently pursuing her Doctorate in Marriage and Family Counseling.

Megan has authored 12 books, and blogs practical marriage and parenting counsel at meganscheibner.com. She hosts the popular Youtube show Thrive Tribe and teaches alongside her husband Steve on the Character Health Youtube channel. She is a sought-after conference speaker, online Bible teacher, and marriage and family counselor. Megan has been a guest on Family Talk with Dr. James Dobson, as well as the Glenn Beck television show.

Megan and her husband Steve share a strong desire to equip today's parents to raise the next generation of Christlike, character healthy leaders. In her spare time, she loves to read, try new

recipes, and cuddle her grandchildren and puppies. Megan enjoys writing, cooking, feeding

teenagers, and everything pertaining to the Boston Red Sox.

More Books by Megan:
- Character Matters: A Daily Step-By-Step Guide To Developing Courageous
Character
- Eight Rules of Communication For Successful Marriages
- An A-Z Guide For Character-Healthy Homeschooling
- In My Seat: A Pilot's Story From Sept.10th-11th.
- Grand Slam: A Four Week Devotional Bible Study For Christian Athletes.
- Rise and Shine: Recipes and Routines For Your Morning.
- Lunch and Literature.
- Dinner and Discipleship.
- Studies in Character.
- 28 Day Discipleship Jumpstart.
- The King of Thing and The Kingdom of Thingdom.
- The Wise Wife: Cause' Wisdom Lasts Longer Than Botox

facebook.com/Character%20Health

twitter.com/CharacterHealth

instagram.com/Characterhealthplus

youtube.com/Character%20Health